WITH COMPLIMENTS OF THE

moody literature mission
for your library's use

This gift was made possible through a special grant by the Family Altar League of Chicago. It is their prayer that this material might assist you in establishing regular family worship in your home.

820 N. LaSalle Street, Chicago, Illinois 60610

CREATIVE FAMILY WORSHIP

DOROTHY MARTIN

MOODY PRESS

CHICAGO

Library of Congress Cataloging in Publication Data

Martin, Dorothy McKay, 1921-
Creative family worship.

1. Family—Religious life. I. Title.

BV4526.2.M29   249   76-8822

ISBN 0-8024-1641-1

Printed in the United States of America

Contents

1

How Important Is the Family?

Now therefore fear the Lord, and serve him in sincerity and in truth: . . . And if it seem evil unto you to serve the Lord, choose you this day whom ye will serve; . . . but as for me and my house, we will serve the Lord (Joshua 24:14-15).

SEVERAL YEARS AGO newspaper headlines screamed stories of the "Manson family"—a group of individuals, many of them young women, who lived together and were dominated by the evil will of one man. We read also of other kinds of communal living, not the traditional idea of a family with father, mother, and children. In these "families" people live together who are not joined by blood ties but by similar interests or goals. For some it is an economic necessity and there is nothing immoral in the arrangement. Others live this way as a gesture of revolt against established customs, particularly the custom of marriage.

Psychologists and sociologists talk a great deal

today about the breakdown of the home and family. Society contributes to this breakdown by approving deviate life-styles, emphasis on sex, and premarital relationships. Uncertainties regarding changing husband-wife roles, the demands of women's lib, the increasing divorce rate, and economic conditions which send both parents out to work put pressures on family life.

People live together openly without benefit of a wedding ceremony and then part as suits their convenience. Some insist this is not wrong because there are no absolute moral standards, and whatever is right for the individual is right regardless of the consequences to others. Many argue that sin, if it exists at all, is just a sickness to be treated. Our materialistic society holds to very little that is absolute.

A permissive attitude toward sex results in wife-swapping and casual living-together arrangements, "trial marriages." Many sneer at marriage as an institution which has been around so long it has outlived its usefulness. It is no longer necessary to have a marriage license as long as two people have a "meaningful relationship."

But God never intended marriage to be a transitory arrangement dissolved at the whim of one or the other of the partners. God ordained marriage as an indissoluble union of two people, valid as long as they lived. The average couple does not realize the permanent sacredness of the vows they exchange.

Even Christians can be swept into forgetting that marriage is a God-ordained, not a human-begun, relationship. God began marriage in the Garden of Eden *before* Adam and Eve sinned, giving it a holy origin. He united the first couple and commanded them to begin a family while they were still in a state of sinlessness, fresh from His creative hand. This foundation lifts marriage out of the mire of selfish convenience; it puts it above the caricature of a "ball and chain" relationship; it invests marriage with a dimension found only in Scripture.

God has never rescinded His command regarding marriage. Instead He reemphasized it through the centuries in His dealings with the human race as He worked through families and used family terms to give spiritual truth. He is our Father! And Jesus, born into a human family, invested marriage and the family with spiritual significance.

Finally Paul, under the Holy Spirit's direction, explained the purpose of marriage. God intended it to illustrate the relationship between Christ and the Church. This purpose was not known in the Garden of Eden or in any succeeding generation until the Church was established after Christ's death, resurrection, and ascension. Then God declared: "For this cause shall a man leave his father and mother, and shall be joined unto his wife, and they two shall be one flesh. This is a great mystery: but I speak concerning Christ and the church" (Ephesians 5:31-32).

Marriage, seen through God's eyes, has a shine and a radiance and a solemnity beyond that given by the temporary candlelight and soft organ music of the ceremony.

When marriage is treated lightly, the home and family are also. The increased use of birth control pills does away with the fear of pregnancy by unmarried girls. And if pregnancy should result, the stigma is removed by the girl either having an abortion or keeping the baby with the approval of society.

The family concept is attacked in many other ways. When Marcia was asked as a little girl what she wanted to be when she grew up, she answered, "A mommy."

She soon learned that not everyone considered this a high enough ambition. Someone always asked scornfully, "Is that all?" or laughed saying, "That's silly! Why don't you want to *be* something?"

Critics of the population explosion lobby vigorously against large families. Advocates of women's liberation give women who prefer to be home with their children a guilt complex because they are not contributing in a worthwhile capacity. The charge comes across loud and clear that a woman who only cares for her home and family is not really *doing* anything.

Totalitarian countries—China in particular—illustrate vividly how a centuries-old way of life can be broken by a determined assault, in this case an assault by the government. The family unit does not exist in China. Instead the country is a gigantic commune, regimented by the dictates of the government. Women are "freed" from the domestic burdens of a home, and child training becomes indoctrination by the state.

This kind of control is not necessarily the goal of those who push for liberating women or of those who advocate day-care centers. Day-care centers are havens for mothers who must work and are desperate for someone to care for their children. But they should be used only from necessity, not as an excuse to avoid the responsibility and care of children. Children need the loving guidance of the family.

Of course, a traditional family with a stay-at-home mother does not necessarily make a good home. Neglected or abused children come from families at every level of society, from poor homes and wealthy, from ignorant and educated. So-called good homes do not always have successful family relationships. The frightful increase in drug use, crime, and runaways among children from homes seeming to have everything going for them is evidence that *things* do not take the place of values.

Even homes where parents profess to be Christians do not automatically have an atmosphere that honors

God. Christian homes can be guilty of neglect, of low standards, of undisciplined children.

The problem is that even the best of families, those where there is harmony and loving concern, are fragmented by many necessary obligations. Both parents and children feel the pressure of activities that are necessary and good. The father's job (and sometimes the mother's), school activities, community and civic meetings, church responsibilities—all of them important—cut into the closeness of family living.

If we want our Christian home to be different, we must care enough to work at preserving individual unity. We must establish priorities for time and interests, show love, set limits that allow for growth, respect each other, and build on God's Word.

This is hard! We cannot put up a wall that will keep out every unwanted influence. A creeping rot of evil infiltrates our homes no matter how we guard against it. Some of this evil is bold and blatant in magazines and books on grocery and drugstore shelves. Some of it comes by sly innuendo in television programs and commercials. Neighbors and friends and relatives come into the home and leave an impression that is different from the standards we set.

Sometimes a negative influence is so gradual but so constant that we are unaware of the rotting danger until it has eaten deeply into the values we are trying to build. We grow accustomed to the ridicule of moral standards in supposedly comic television programs, with their sly, vulgar jokes. High recommendations of filthy books and movies gradually dull our sensitivity to their dirt. Long ago Alexander Pope said:

> Vice is a monster of so frightful mein
> As to be hated, needs but to be seen;
> Yet seen too oft, familiar with her face,
> We first endure, then pity, then embrace.

Our home must safeguard our children against becoming too familiar with evil. It must be the first line of defense against the devil, because it is the first influence children have.

But how to do this is the problem. We can turn off the television set, refuse to buy certain magazines or books, and give guidelines by which to measure values. And yet, children cannot be sheltered from every contact with the world—and they should not be. A hothouse plant does not survive long outside its protected environment. How foolish it would be to give a sixteen-year-old the keys to a car and turn him loose on a busy expressway without any driving experience. He would be a menace to himself and other drivers. He needs a competent driver to give both education and experience.

It is hard to achieve the right balance. Some parents overprotect their children; others are too permissive. But we must give children some protection from evil and some standards by which they can judge between right and wrong, good and evil. They must learn at home by instruction and example how to live as Titus 2:12 commands: "soberly, righteously, and godly, in this present world."

Children are not born with the ability to live this command; parents have to help them learn. And children have a right to expect this kind of help, just as they have a right to expect that parents will feed and clothe and educate them. These are not things parents do as extras; they are duties we owe our children in every part of their life.

But sometimes parents justifiably feel like the two Boy Scouts who tried to help a little old lady across the street. When they reported their good deed to the scout leader, he asked why it took two of them to help one elderly person. They answered, "Because she didn't want to go."

Children do not always walk willingly in the way they should go. We who are committed to raising children according to God's pattern of holiness sometimes have to make them walk the way we point.

Child-education authorities have long agreed that the parents and the home are the key to childhood development and adjustment to life. It is the home that shapes and molds, for children know only the home atmosphere in those first critical months when attitudes form which have lasting effects throughout life.

God established the home to meet the deepest needs humans have—for love, security, discipline, self-respect, and spiritual nourishment. The Holy Spirit illustrated this as He told of Jesus' growth in Luke 2:52: "And Jesus increased in wisdom [mental] and stature [physical], and in favour with God [spiritual] and man [social]." The home is responsible for children's growth in these same four areas.

Except in the tragic cases of child neglect or abuse, parents teach necessary skills very early in life. We teach each child to feed and dress himself, to brush teeth and hair, and to make his bed. He is sent to school, and his homework is checked. He is encouraged to develop friendships and trained to be polite. All this early training lays the foundation for later skills.

Good physical and mental health *is* a heritage to be prized. After examining a patient, a doctor remarked on her good physical condition but said, "You can't take any credit for it. You got it from your ancestors."

Can't we expect that good spiritual health should also be a heritage? Not that salvation can be passed on from one generation to the next. It is impossible to inherit faith; each one must decide for Christ himself. But the spiritual atmosphere in a home in one generation is important to the generation yet unborn. Paul speaks of Timothy's faith, "which dwelt first

in thy grandmother Lois, and thy mother Eunice"
(2 Timothy 1:5).

Parents can begin a gradual process of giving the
"milk" of the Word (1 Peter 2:2) to help the child
grow until he can handle the "strong meat" of the
Word (Hebrews 5:12). Doing nothing to train children spiritually is not just neglect; it is actively building a vacuum which has to be filled with something.
Whether negative or positive, training constantly
takes place as children grow. Childhood is a con-
tinual learning process, either for good or against it.

Raising children "in the nurture and admonition of
the Lord" as God reminds us in Ephesians 6:4 is a
job that begins with the child's birth and is an all-day
and everyday responsibility. Christina Rossetti's
poignant verse reminds us:

> Does the road wind up-hill all the way?
>   Yes, to the very end.
> Will the day's journey take the whole long day?
>   From morn to night, my friend.

Training children to love and live for God is this
kind of a journey. But it is worth it!

Parents cannot do the work of the Holy Spirit in
the lives of their children. Only He can make them
know they are sinners and need Christ's righteousness
(John 16:8-11). We cannot make spiritual choices
for our children or take the step of salvation for them.
We cannot guarantee that they will live godly lives.

Unbelieving parents have children who become Christians, while Christian parents have children who grow up unbelieving.

Children of believing parents *ought* to become Christians, even though we cannot make them do so. But we do have the responsibility of providing an atmosphere in the home which will daily point them to God. We can put before them the whole counsel of God, "line upon line" (Isaiah 28:10), in day-by-day living.

We must remember that a home is judged by the product it turns out. So a Christian home should turn out people who reflect a standard of what a Christian home should be. Such a home and family has a "salting" effect on the community. Salt in the right proportions improves food and brings out the flavor. The Scripture says that believers have the effect on their generation of keeping sin from being as bad as it would be if they were not there.

How does this work in a practical way? Do other people clean up their language when they talk to you? Does a neighbor shove an indecent magazine under a sofa pillow when you come to visit? These reactions should not be because you draw away in shocked horror; that is not the right salting effect. A Christian's life should be so clear and joyous and transparently pure that a neighbor, even when he does not adopt that kind of life, will be uncomfortable about his own standards.

A Christian home must exemplify attitudes of honesty, hospitality, concern, courtesy, and graciousness. These are more impressive to unbelieving neighbors than perfect attendance at Sunday school for twenty-five years without those qualities. A Christian family which has quarreling, disobedient children, shouting parents, and unpleasant relations with neighbors mocks the name of Christ.

Louise Matthews made that mistake without meaning to. She went from door to door each week, urging neighbors to come to a Bible study. But she could often be heard screaming at her children because they had not washed the dishes or vacuumed the carpet—which most of the neighbors thought were her jobs, anyway.

The Richardsons took off punctually for Sunday school and prayer meeting every week. But they always had an overflowing garbage can with sacks and bottles spilling over onto their neighbor's property.

Bert Anderson put a tract in every letter he wrote but left borrowed garden tools out to rust.

You see, a Christian home carries a double burden of responsibility: to have internal family relationships that bind its members in close, loving fellowship with each other and with God; and external relationships that will attract neighbors to the Lord Jesus for salvation.

How can we accomplish this? What can we do so that neighbors looking on will say, "What makes

them love each other?" We can raise children to
walk with the Lord day by day through each year.

How is this possible? By following God's methods
outlined in His Word and bringing the family to God
every day for His blessing. This is what the family
altar can do if we really work at it.

2

Parents at the Altar

And these words, which I command thee this day, shall be in thine heart: And thou shalt teach them diligently unto thy children, and shalt talk of them when thou sittest in thine house, and when thou walkest by the way, and when thou liest down, and when thou risest up (Deuteronomy 6:6-7).

PATTY MARRIED the day after she graduated from high school and a year later had triplets. "Nobody ever told me marriage was like *this!*" she wailed as she looked at the little, red-faced, squalling bits of humanity for which she and Bill were now responsible.

Fortunately, newly married couples are not usually blessed so overwhelmingly! But before we are married, most of us have very little training in being a good parent, partly because we are not interested in the subject until we suddenly *are* parents. Generally in this area we learn by doing. Some learn quickly and do a good job; others muddle along somehow; a few fail tragically. But all of us make mistakes—including Christian parents.

It is sadly true that godly parents do not automatically have godly children. Scripture illustrates this all too vividly. Eli was a priest, a servant of God. Yet God said, "I will judge his house for ever for the iniquity which he knoweth; because his sons made themselves vile, and he restrained them not" (1 Samuel 3:11). And David, whom God called "a man after his own heart" (Acts 13:22), lost his children to evil living and disdain of God's laws. Everyone can cite examples of this, some from within their own family circle.

Is there any way we can guarantee the salvation and spiritual growth of our children? No. But God does give principles we can follow. The verse which heads this chapter says: "And these words . . . *shall be in thine heart.*" That is the first requirement. Raising a child to be a man of God begins with the parent. We cannot communicate what we do not have. We do communicate what we are. Before we can help our children love and obey God, we must first be loving and obeying Him. This is possible only if we have new life through faith in Jesus Christ.

If you are concerned about your children and want the best for them, but you do not know Jesus Christ as your personal Saviour from sin, this is the place to start. You must first trust Jesus Christ as your Saviour and take God's free offer of salvation. God's invitation is very clear:

> For God so loved the world, that he gave his only begotten Son, that whosoever believeth in him should not perish, but have everlasting life (John 3:16).

> Neither is there salvation in any other: for there is none other name under heaven given among men, whereby we must be saved (Acts 4:12).

When your relationship to God is established and you are His child, then you can begin to grow before your children and communicate to them their need of Jesus Christ.

As soon as a Christian home begins, a husband and wife should share what each has personally discovered in God's Word, for God reveals Himself to the one who seeks Him. This is the family altar.

But we really need three separate times of devotions for three separate purposes. One is the personal quiet time, when *I* come before God, needing answers to *my* prayers, help for *my* problems, wisdom for *my* questions, strength for *my* weakness. I must individually, all alone, confess personal sin and renew commitment of my life. This is what the individual quiet time does. God speaks clearly to the individual heart and opens His Word and gives the ability to "comprehend with all saints what is the breadth, and length, and depth, and height; and to know the love of Christ, which passeth knowledge, that ye might be filled with all the fulness of God" (Ephesians 3:18-19). The only requirement is that we really *want* this knowledge. When we do, our experience will be like that of Jeremiah: "Thy words were found, and I did eat them; and thy word was unto me the joy and rejoicing of mine heart" (Jeremiah 15:16). When husband and wife each has something from the Lord, then the family altar can be a sharing together from the richness of a personal encounter with God.

This leads into a second time of devotions, when parents jointly pray for their children. When we pray together for our children, we pour our hearts out to God in special, loving intercession for them—His gifts to us. We name each one individually, his dearness, his special qualities, his weaknessess, his strengths, his need of salvation and spiritual growth. We yield each one to God for His protection and guidance, giving them back to Him daily in a loving surrender of these precious jewels. Of course, these devotional times always include prayer also for personal needs, family problems, relatives, missionaries, and the church.

We are all affected to some degree by the agitation for women's equality. There *are* inequalities which should be corrected, but not by throwing out the scriptural order of the relationship in the home. The husband is the head of the wife, and both are in submission to God. The devotional time is the ultimate place of equality. Here the truth of Scripture is clearly seen that there is "neither male nor female" (Galatians 3:28). For in the family altar both husband and wife share what God has given them separately.

When parents have established these two times of devotions, then they see more clearly how much they need a family altar. They can say to their children, "We've found something so important to us, that missing it is like missing a meal—we get hungry! And we want to share it with you."

It is hard to start a family altar after children come if the parents do not have the habit already established. A family altar a *habit?* Yes! There is nothing wrong with a habit. We all have perfectly good habits which take us through every day. But the family altar habit has eternal consequences. By it we say with the psalmist, "Oh how love I thy law! It is my meditation all the day. . . . How sweet are thy words unto my taste! Yea, sweeter than honey to my mouth" (Psalm 119:97, 103). How important is a family altar to parents? What does it do for them?

A family altar helps parents obey God in their daily living. No parent has a right to say to his child, "This is the way, walk ye in it" (Isaiah 30:21) if he does not walk that way himself.

Holiness in the home starts with the parents' personal convictions. Before the children are born, parents must have an ingrained standard of personal purity. The father who laughs halfheartedly at a dirty story told by a friend, "just to be polite," sets a double standard of values for his son. A mother who avidly follows the stories on afternoon television endorses, just by her interest, a way of life which totally disregards God's laws.

If we do not have definite, settled convictions about the authority of God's Word, we cannot instill in our children confidence about its reliability. If we do not show by experience that we believe God's Word, "Let not your heart be troubled; neither let it be afraid" (John 14:27), we lead our children to doubt God's ability to care for them. We can only say the words of 1 Corinthians 11:1, "Be ye followers of me," if we can honestly say the rest of the verse, "even as I also am of Christ." *We* have to obey God in *our* daily experience and let our children see our obedience.

Children sometimes think they are the only ones who have to obey. "When *I* grow up, I won't have to do what anyone tells me," said Billy, in the mistaken idea of what being an adult means.

Men in the business world face constant temptations which could cause disobedience to God's commands. When a man is pressured by the need to make good in order to provide for his family and faced with constant demands to compromise or shade the truth, he needs the moral strength a family altar

gives. He can go into the demands of his job with
his wife's prayers going with him in the specific situations he shared with her in the time of family prayer.
And a wife coping with young children and trying to
live Christ before the older children, helping a neighbor, carrying a part-time job, can do so with the
serenity that comes from a time spent with her husband in prayer. Each family member prays not for
generalities but for definite needs of others in the
family and receives the same kind of support in return.

*A family altar binds husband and wife in a loving
relationship.* One of the essential needs in any home
is clear and open communication among family
members, and this must begin with the parents. Each
one can think the other has the best of the marriage
deal. The wife may complain that her husband has
the stimulation of being with adults, while she is
stuck in the four walls of the house, with only preschoolers for company; he that she can set her own
schedule without the pressure to meet deadlines.
When this is their attitude, her perfunctory, "How
was your day?" receives his, "So-so. What about
you?" But there is no sincere interest or caring on
the part of either.

God wants Christian homes to have a climate of
love and trust and forgiveness. Love must be the
surrounding atmosphere—husband and wife for each

other, parents and children for each other. And the love must be expressed both in words and actions.

A family altar keeps before a couple the richness of all that they have in Christ Jesus. It reminds them of their responsibility to be partakers of the grace of God. The family altar is one means God can use to transform marriage into the splendidly colored mosaic of Galatians 5:22-23, with love, joy, peace, longsuffering, gentleness, goodness, meekness, and self-control combining to complete the picture of happiness.

The family altar helps parents obey God's commands regarding raising children. When God created the world, He did not leave it to run itself. Instead, He set laws in operation which control and sustain the universe under His direction. The laws of gravity, of molecular division, and so on, were not invented by man; he simply discovered them as he observed the universe.

When God established the family, He ordained certain laws to keep the family world rotating in its proper orbit. One of these laws governs the relationships in the family. The husband is the head of the wife, the wife is in submission to him, and the children are obedient to their parents. But all are to be subject to God. Today's advocates of women's liberation are wrong to think this principle makes one partner superior and the other inferior. The husband

and wife each has his own place to fill. Putting the husband at the head of the home is simply God's pattern for an orderly, smoothly working family relationship.

Another of God's laws for the family's orderly working is that parents are to "train up a child in the way he should go: and when he is old, he will not depart from it" (Proverbs 22:6).

This is an area where we must all tread lightly and with prayer, to avoid the extremes of either judging or excusing ourselves or others. Those whose children are grown and continue to walk with God and have established their own Christian homes dare not sit in judgment on any other family. No parent can take credit to himself. He must always say, "It was the grace of God"—because it is *always* God's grace that saves and keeps any of us.

It is not easy to raise children. How do we know when to yield and when to stand firm? Is Susy's temper tantrum a phase she will outgrow; or is it deliberate, willful disobedience? Or is it the result of a physical problem? How much should Margie play at Beth's house, where there is no Christian influence? Jack has begun to lie consistently—what should we do? Sometimes a husband and wife cannot agree on how to handle these and similar situations.

Child-training theories come and go, but psychologists and educators return periodically to the view the Bible holds consistently—that discipline is necessary in raising children. This does not mean discipline only in the narrow sense of punishment. Discipline is much more than that. It is training children in the total growing process of becoming mature persons in God's family. Discipline includes all the means and influences parents use to train children to walk in the narrow path that leads to life everlasting. Sometimes the discipline is a spanking or depriving of some privilege. Sometimes it is forgiving a wrongdoing—not overlooking or excusing it, but forgiving. Of course, always, *always* discipline must be carried out in love, even when it involves punishment.

We do not discipline our children for our own convenience, or to make them a credit to us, or to conform them to our standards. We do it to bring them into the place Romans 12:1-2 commands: "Present your bodies a living sacrifice, holy, acceptable unto God. . . . be ye transformed by the renewing of your mind, that ye may prove what is that good, and acceptable, and perfect, will of God."

Those who think being a parent is not very important should think through the implications of the verse that heads this chapter and the warning of Ephesians 6:4: "Ye fathers, provoke not your children to wrath: but bring them up in the nurture and admonition of the Lord." God sees our responsibility as a total commitment of thought and effort that covers *all* of life's actions, from getting up in the morning, through all the activities of the day, up to and including going to bed at night. Discipline is a matter of personal living inside the home and of witness to others in actions outside the home.

This total commitment is possible only as we feel its urgency. The Word of God and prayer must be to parents as the experience the prophet Jeremiah wrote of: "Then I said, I will not make mention of him, nor speak any more in his name. But his word was in mine heart as a burning fire shut up in my bones, and I was weary with forbearing, and I could not stay" (Jeremiah 20:9). If we do not have this desire for God's Word, we will never be able to follow its instructions in raising our children.

God gives a strong warning in 1 Timothy 5:8 about the one who does not take care of the material needs of his own family but leaves them to the mercy of others. Such a one, God says, "hath denied the faith, and is worse than an infidel."

Few Christian parents would neglect their children's physical and material needs. Yet they do something far worse by neglecting spiritual needs. Often this is not a deliberate refusal to have a family altar or establish other regular habits of prayer and Bible reading. The neglect is usually the result of the "cares of this world," which take up time.

Job said, "I have esteemed the words of his mouth more than my necessary food" (23:12). When *we* have this sense of the importance of God's Word, it will be caught by our children. Remember, the word must first be "in *thine* heart" (Deuteronomy 6:6).

A family altar keeps parents alert to the questions and doubts their children may have. When children leave the shelter of the home for the world of school and neighborhood and friends, they quickly discover that not everyone has the same values and standards they were taught.

Tom blurted one evening, "The guys in school all laughed at me when I said Adam and Eve were real people who really lived in the Garden of Eden. They were, weren't they, Dad? The Bible says so, doesn't it?"

On the surface it is a trivial matter, but important in the long run if Dad takes time—and knows how—to help Tom understand that his faith in the Bible is not misplaced. The family altar can be used by parents to open the Bible to their children and find answers to questions from the God of all wisdom.

But too often we are afraid to do this because *we* are afraid the Bible will not stand the test. The parent who draws back in shocked surprise when his child expresses a doubt often does so because he is uncertain about his own trust in God's Word. So he loses a precious moment of communication between himself and his child and, even worse, plants a doubt about God's reliability in his child's mind.

The question Tom was asking was basically, "Can I trust the Bible?" and the answer is a very positive yes! And not just "Yes, because I say so," as a parent, but "Yes, because it has been proven reliable beyond a doubt many, many times." We can always confidently say, "The Bible *is* God's Word, and you don't have to try to defend it." Then the family altar can initiate a time of searching for more information about the Bible and lay a firm basis for turning to the Word when other questions and doubts come.

Isn't this partially fulfilling the promise "and when he is old he will not depart"?

The family altar gives parents new perspectives on problems. This business of living together is not all sweetness and light. Demanding one's own rights, selfishness, quarreling, disrespect, a lack of love— all these too often characterize Christian homes and tear the family to shreds. Sometimes neither parents nor children are willing to listen to the other side and see the other person's viewpoint.

Joe and Helen were desperate about the bitterness that ate at their two preteen daughters. No amount of punishing or talking to the girls helped. Then they began to pray for their daughters in their own devotional time. Next they talked openly about the situation one evening in family devotions and discovered that part of the problem lay in their own attitude toward the girls. They had reacted to the quarreling in a harsh, arbitrary manner which had only caused more friction between the sisters and made them unwilling to listen to advice. The parents' readiness to admit they were wrong and needed to change their attitude gradually helped dissolve the bitterness between the girls.

The family altar helps parents love their children. Oh, we do love them, of course. We provide for them, shelter them, educate them, kiss them—we *love* them. But when we pray for them, we love them in a special way—a forgiving, yearning way.

It is difficult to remain angry or carry a grudge when we have brought a problem to the Lord openly with a contrite, broken plea for His forgiveness and help. How much we need to live 1 Thessalonians 2:8 before our children: "So being affectionately desirous of you, we were willing to have imparted unto you, not the gospel of God only, but also our own souls, because ye were dear to us." It is the "love of God . . . shed abroad in our hearts" (Romans 5:5) that makes it possible for any of us to have love and show it, even—or especially—in unlovely situations and to those who do not act in a loving way. The quieting influence of the family altar can do this. It is the place to be open in relationships and express our love for the children who are so dear to us.

The family altar is the place for parents to express their need of help. Carl thought that his responsibility as a father was to show only his strengths to his family. In the process, the anxieties and pressures of his job exploded on his family as he jumped on them for every little irritating thing they did. Finally he realized this and asked their forgiveness, explaining his actions. He gained new respect from his twelve-year-old son, who said, "Dad, I didn't think you ever worried about anything. I'm sure glad you're like me!"

Children do need the security of parents who are strong and resourceful. But they must see them also as sinners who have been redeemed by God and are in constant need of His grace—and willing to admit their need.

As a family comes unitedly to the family altar, God gives the individual guidance each one needs. He has given a terrific promise in James 1:5-6: "If any of you lack wisdom, let him ask of God, that giveth to all men liberally, and upbraideth not; and it shall be given him. But let him ask in faith, nothing wavering." This verse gives us hope! We all need wisdom; not one of us can go it alone. And we especially need this wisdom from God.

As we ask for definite help in specific situations— the practical, everyday matters of training in personal cleanliness; doing well in school; getting along with people; working without complaining; learning honesty, self-control, love for others—God gives the wisdom needed for this training.

More than that, according to this verse, He gives wisdom beyond what is needed for the particular moment. He gives "liberally." Perhaps this means the wisdom from one problem can be used in other similar situations; He will bring the resource to mind again as we need it later. This is part of His doing "exceeding abundantly above all that we can ask or think" (Ephesians 3:20). And beyond all this, the verse says He gives without scolding us for not having wisdom: He "upbraideth not."

We need to learn this in handling our children. We expect more from them than they are capable of and then scold them for not living up to what we expect. We say, "You're old enough to know better!" or "Don't act like a baby!" God does not do that. He is loving and longsuffering to His children.

The family altar gives the father opportunity to fulfill his place as the spiritual leader of the home. Some men cannot take the spiritual leadership because they are not spiritual; other men will not take it. Some unsaved husbands are indifferent to the matter and do not object to the wife and children praying together. Others actively oppose the whole idea of family prayers. God has a word for women in this situation in 1 Peter 3:1: "Likewise, ye wives, be in subjection to your own husbands; that, if any obey not the word, they also may without the word be won by the conversation [behavior] of the wives."

But what about the spiritual training of the children in the meantime? Trust God for them also. They are more dear to Him even than they are to us.

He will make a way so the children will not suffer, if their mother is faithful in her private praying for her husband and children.

But God specifically put the father in the home as the priest of the family with instructions to *him* to teach his children diligently. The man who abdicates this privilege does it against God's express command and cheats himself and his family.

Of course this does not mean that the rest of the family should just sit around and wait for Dad to do it all. As we will see in later chapters, the family altar is a *family* project, with everyone taking part in talking and sharing and making discoveries. This makes it the best part of the whole day!

3

What Do Children Get out of It?

But continue thou in the things which thou hast learned and been assured of, knowing of whom thou hast learned them; and that from a child thou hast known the holy scriptures, which are able to make thee wise unto salvation through faith which is in Christ Jesus (2 Timothy 3:14-15).

THE SHOWER Barb's friends gave before her first baby came brought squeals of delight as she opened each package of dainty, hand-knit sweaters or practical gifts of diapers and baby bottles. The square package from one friend was a large, easy-to-read Bible with beautiful, colored pictures.

"For use in your family altar," read the words on the card.

"Thanks, but it'll be a long time before Junior can sit through family devotions," Barb answered as she laughed.

"When do you plan to start feeding him?"

"Well—right away, of course."

"Then that's when you should start feeding him God's Word," her friend insisted.

No, not by reading a chapter and saying a long prayer the day you come home from the hospital. You will start in a little way, because the baby is little. Our daughter put her baby's tiny hands together for a moment and said, "Thank you, God," for the very first bottle. Such a small beginning! But a year later, Bethany folded her own hands and waited for the prayer.

The verse at the beginning of this chapter says knowing God's Word can help a child be saved. If we hold off having family devotions because the children are too young to sit still, or wait until the children are old enough to read with understanding, we will find we have waited too long.

A mother asked a minister when she should start teaching her five-year-old about God. "Madam, you are already five years too late," came his quick reply.

The family altar is a natural place for a child to be told about Jesus. God told parents to teach His Word to their children. We know our children better than any teacher can. Sometimes we foolishly overlook faults or explain away mistakes, and this is wrong.

But we know their personalities and strengths and weaknesses. We know that Johnny is enthusiastic and dependable; that Peter is quick to start a job but does not always carry through; that Mary believes everything she is told, while Ruth automatically asks why. And so we treat them differently and explain salvation in different ways. Mary may accept Jesus as her Saviour simply and quietly, without doubt. Ruth may have to question, "How do I know?" and "Why did Jesus have to die?" and "How can I be sure?"

One thing we can be sure of is that children can know that God loves them and that they can love Him. John 3:16 is a verse that is beyond the comprehension of the wisest person. Yet the simplicity of the truth: "God so loved the world, that he gave his only begotten Son, that whosoever believeth in him should not perish, but have everlasting life" can be understood by a young child.

Maybe this is because children need love and respond to it. We do not need a psychologist to tell us that. But studies do show that how children develop later in life is tied in with how much love they received as infants.

Because children respond to love, we do not have to hesitate to tell them about the Lord Jesus' love for them. God sets no age limit on salvation, and neither should we. Jesus said about children, "Forbid them not, to come unto me" (Matthew 19:14). If we do not give them the opportunity to accept Christ, we *are* forbidding them.

At the same time we must be careful not to push them into saying they accept Christ without helping

them understand what salvation is. Some of the opportunities we give may be in little bits and pieces,
like the sudden exclamation Mother makes to Susie
as they pick up toys, "I'm *so* glad Jesus loves us,
aren't you?" But salvation can also be made very
plain in the family devotion time and outlined in four
simple steps: (1) God loves people—John 3:16;
(2) all have done wrong—Romans 3:23; (3) God
loves us so much He sent Jesus to die for us—1 Corinthians 15:3-4; and (4) those who ask Jesus to be
their Saviour will belong to His family forever—
John 1:12.

None of us should dare question the fact that a
young child can be saved. Five-year-old Dottie did
not raise her hand when other children responded to
an invitation in a children's meeting where the Gospel had been clearly explained. Her parents did not
want to push her, but they did want to make sure
she had understood, and they questioned her that
evening. She answered, "I didn't have to raise my
hand because I already said yes to Jesus in bed one
night."

There was a lot she did not understand, and there
was a lot of "growing in grace" that was yet to come.
But she never lost the certainty of her place as a
child of God.

This certainty does not come as early or as readily
to every child and you may have both a Mary—who
accepts easily—and a Ruth—who questions—in

your family. So use the family altar time to repeat the salvation opportunity and to give assurance.

Sarah had asked Jesus to come into her heart several times—once in family worship, another time in vacation Bible school, and still another time in her Sunday school class. Finally as a fourth grader she came to her mother in tears, not sure she was a Christian. Her mother looked up Bible verses with her and reminded her of her earlier responses. Then she said, "Just to be sure, we'll kneel down right now and you ask Jesus to be your Saviour. Then we'll write the date in your Bible, and if you have any doubt about it later, this will remind you." And so Sarah was happily sure that she belonged to God.

Her mother might have reacted, "Of course you're a Christian! God doesn't want you to doubt Him." And Sarah would have struggled on, not sure and afraid to ask again.

But being saved and knowing it is just the seed planted. Then cames growth, which usually requires some help—weeding and watering and protecting.

So the family altar gives instruction in righteousness. What does this mean to children? Sitting quietly while father reads a list of commands from the Bible?

No. It is Kevin's learning not to hit back when he is teased, *because* God says, "Be ye kind one to another, tenderhearted, forgiving one another," *because* "God for Christ's sake hath forgiven you"

(Ephesians 4:32). It is Lucy not banging the dishes around when she has to do them before playing, *because* God said, "Do all things without murmurings and disputing" (Philippians 2:14). It is learning how to share when you do not want to, to do a job without being reminded, to obey when you do not see why you must.

The family altar is the place where the commands of God to live a holy life are read and discussed in concrete terms. God's command not to lie seems to be clear-cut. We should not have any trouble obeying it, and yet we all do. These problems can be talked about honestly in the family circle. Is there a difference in degrees of lies? Isn't it sometimes kinder to lie than to tell the truth (this business, you know, about not hurting someone's feelings)? Do we have to confess *every* lie? To everyone?

There will not be freedom of discussion in a family altar time if principles are given in heavy-handed parental lecturing. There must be mutual sharing, where all stand together in need of prayer. Dad shows he needs help as he says, "I wish you'd all help me. I'm supposed to cover for the boss and say he's in conference when he's really out playing golf. What do you think I should do?" The kids see that Dad faces the same kind of problems they do.

So the family altar becomes a binding adhesive of mutual concern that no amount of stern, "If you tell one more lie, I'm going to spank you!" can create.

You see, a family devotional time is more than just reading the Bible without comment and praying, though even that is valuable and better than not doing anything at all. But it can be so much more as the Word of God comes alive in the experience of each one in the family.

"I hate Ralph!" Mike yells as he slams into the house. If Mother says, her voice sharp and critical, "You're a Christian, and it's wrong to say that," Mike will go off, still mad, to find his brother and punch him.

But Mother can say sympathetically, "We all feel that way sometimes. What happened?" Together they talk about the problem, and Mike can be reminded of God's Word, "If a man say, I love God, and hateth his brother, he is a liar; for he that loveth not his brother whom he hath seen, how can he love God whom he hath not seen?" (1 John 4:20).

"Resist the devil, and he will flee from you" (James 4:7) has a basic idea, but it comes across to people at different levels of meaning. For the toddler it is the "No-no" of the books on the shelf or the sparkling glass objects on the étagère. When he gets near them and shakes his head without touching them, he does not know he is resisting the devil—but he is! This is just as real a temptation to him as those that will come later, and the ability he has to resist later depends on what happens when he is still a two-year-old.

As God's Word is read and put to work in daily life, we understand more of it. We do not want to remain babies, constantly needing the "no-no" reminders. Parents and children together can grow in wanting to obey God and know what the Bible means by the "riches of his grace" (Ephesians 2:7).

Then the family altar can nourish children in God's Word. This sounds dull. And many people think being a Christian means not having any fun. Even Christians think this sometimes, and maybe a lot of us give other people the impression that we are not very happy. But that is because we do not know the Bible as we should, for it shows Christianity as alive and glowing and happy—"Blessed is the man" who follows Me, God says (see Psalm 1).

Sometimes parents think that a "be good or God won't like you" concept should be developed. Absolutely not! This is contrary to Scripture—first, because that is not the way God is. The way He acts does not depend on the way we act. He is always the same, regardless of how we behave toward Him. In the second place, none of us can ever deserve God's approval. We cannot be good enough for Him to like us; He loves us even though we are not good. The Bible says this very clearly: "Even when we were dead in sins" (Ephesians 2:5)—and therefore absolutely unable to do good or be good—Christ died for us, "the just for the unjust, that he might bring us to God" (1 Peter 3:18).

We must always show God to our children in His loving, forgiving character, and with it His absolute holiness.

Let's never forget that God gave us the Bible "for doctrine, for reproof, for correction, for instruction in righteousness" (2 Timothy 3:16) in order that we will grow to be like Christ. Do we use it that way and for that purpose? The family altar time lays the basic foundation for later understanding of the deep doctrinal truths of the Christian faith:

1. God is the Creator of the world and Ruler of the universe. But the little child learns of Him at home as the One who loves him. And even this can be understood just a little at a time.

    "How can God know about me, when He isn't here with me?" Sue asked when she undressed for bed one evening.

    And her mother explained, "Well, when I close the door and sit out in the living room, I'm thinking about you and loving you, even though you can't see me. If I can do that, God can too, because He's greater than I am."

2. Jesus is the coming King of kings and Lord of lords. But to the little child He is the baby in the manger and Someone who grew up and loves him.

3. Sin is a deliberate turning from God's way and choosing to walk one's own way. The child does

not know the theological implications of the sin nature he inherited from Adam. But he does know that when Mother says, "Don't touch that," he wants to touch it; when Dad says, "You can't have it," he wants it. The family altar training will help him grow up to choose God's way.

4. The Holy Spirit is the third Person of the Trinity and equally God with the Father and the Son. This is a truth little children cannot understand. But little by little, He can be spoken of as we speak of God and tell children that the Holy Spirit is a Friend who will help them obey God. When they do not understand, you can say, "I don't either. But the Bible tells me the Holy Spirit is my Helper, so I know He is."

5. The Church, according to Ephesians, is the body of Christ. To children it is a place—a place they go to happily when they are little, but when they get older they sometimes ask *why* they have to go.

Should children be made to go to church? Well, not made, exactly—but helped to want to go. We can teach our children that the church is not a building only, but a family of believers in Christ who love and care for each other. We should want to be together now, because someday we will all be together with God, and we will be "holy and without blemish" (Ephesians 5:27), which means there will not be anything wrong with us.

Use the family altar time to find out how the Church began (Acts 2), its history (why there are so many different groups), how it grew. Why do we have the Lord's Supper? Why do we baptize? Is the offering like paying dues? What do we do to become members? How *are* we the body of Christ?

Stretch the family altar time to enrich your children's knowledge and appreciation of God and His Word.

Let your family time develop a love for spiritual things. Never let it be a time of forced listening to the Bible, of unwilling participation, of grim endurance of family "togetherness" while something much more fun beckons in the next room or outside. Parents can make this a special time of hearing God speak. The entire fabric of your children's growing years can be woven through with the rich threads of love for God and His Word.

It takes time and effort to do this. You will have to develop attitudes and search out methods that will appeal to all the age levels and interests. Some ideas will be suggested in a later chapter. Just remember that the family altar will only be as important to your children as it is to you.

The family altar gives children a reason for obedience. Many times we give commands to our children and are met with objections and excuses until we explode, "Do what I tell you without arguing!"

We could avoid some of this if we understood the

purpose of discipline. It is not punishment only, though we know discipline does include punishment. The goal of discipline is to take children from the parents' outer control to an inner self-control. We want to move them from the doing-because-they-are-made-to, to the doing-because-they-ought-(and want)-to. Anyone can make a child be quiet by tying him to a chair and gagging him. Or he can be made to be quiet by giving him something so engrossing that his attention is riveted. We want to use the family altar to help our children shift from external controls to control by inner conviction.

The open intimacy of the family worship time can be used to teach children what it means to obey God. The basic principles of Romans and Corinthians that we are free only as we submit to God are difficult to understand. But they do need to be discussed and explained. If possible, find ways to illustrate them in terms the children can understand.

Sometimes an illustration comes almost by accident. Jenny's mother found her in tears one day, with two limp goldfish on the floor beside her. "I only wanted to give them more room than they've got in the bowl," Jenny cried. Her mother explained that the fish belonged in the water. They were only safe—and so, free—when they were in the place God had made for them. She and Jenny shared the incident that evening in devotions.

The family altar can give the "armor" to protect

children from unbelief. The Bible has always been the focal point of Satan's attacks in every age. Unbelief questions the historicity of the Bible, its facts, its inspiration, its accuracy, its value. This is done by outright criticism and by subtle ridicule.

But in the circle of a loving family concerned for each other's growth, we may face issues honestly and find answers by talking them over with each other and with God. Children can be free to ask questions, express doubts, and seek answers without being jumped on by parents reacting in shock to the doubts.

Tom asked his question about creation out of honest bewilderment. If his dad evaded or ignored it or answered out of ignorance, Tom would wonder if the Bible was wrong. When these questions come, we must answer carefully. This is no time to pretend knowledge.

All this lifts the family altar from a rushed, ten-minute, tacked-on-at-the-end-of-a-busy-day time. Instead, it is a vital part of the whole day's experience. Mother reads a good illustration and clips it to share with the family. In the office, the man whom Dad has been talking to says, "You know, the Bible is finally beginning to make sense to me"; and Dad thinks, "I've got to tell the kids that tonight, since they've been praying for this fellow." A question comes up in school, and the children mentally file it away to ask in family worship.

Help children think critically. Let them know

they do not have to believe something just because it is in a school textbook. For instance, talk through evolution with them at home. Be careful in this—be sure you know that more is involved in it than just the "we're descended from monkeys" idea. Discuss other subjects—the cults, Yoga, how nonviolence fits in with the Bible's teaching. The family altar becomes a time of study and research and thought that goes beyond the actual time spent in worship. It is integrated into all of life.

Does this sound ideal? Yes, of course—and perhaps it is. We will discuss specific, practical ways of teaching the Bible in chapter 6. But let's not forget that we are talking about the "line upon line" teaching that God wants our children to have. If we are faithful, we can dare to trust God to give our children the stamina to stand boldly for Him.

The family altar provides protection from evil. I have read about a small plant that grows in a coal mine. Even though it is completely surrounded by the clinging grime of the coal dust, the plant's leaves keep their pure whiteness because they are coated with a waxy substance that makes the dust slide off.

We have growing plants in our families—our children. And we long for them to grow up pure and "unspotted from the world" (James 1:27). Well, faith in God's holy Book can surround them with a sheen of assurance that God's way is right. We can help them learn to say, "I will fear no evil: for thou art with me" (Psalm 23:4).

But many children grow up in homes where a family altar is kept faithfully, and yet they do not carry it over into their own homes. How can you and I keep this from happening in our children's experience? One way is by making the family time a happy time, but it should not be in a fun-and-games way so that children remember only the *fun* and not the God around whom the happy time was built. We want the family altar to be a "one of the best things our family did" memory. Then they will want to build their family on the stability and trust in God that guarded their growing years.

If the family altar is to be this kind of memory, it has to be more than a perfunctory observance that we keep only if time allows, or if it is convenient for everyone, or if there is nothing more exciting to do.

We can help our children enjoy family worship so much that it becomes a necessary part of their lives. Let's help our children say: "Teach me thy way, O LORD; I will walk in thy truth: unite my heart to fear thy name. I will praise thee, O Lord my God, with all my heart: and I will glorify thy name for evermore" (Psalm 86:11-12).

4

Goals for the Family Altar

*All Scripture is given by inspiration of God, and is
profitable for doctrine, for reproof, for correction,
for instruction in righteousness: that the man of
God may be perfect, throughly furnished unto all
good works* (2 Timothy 3:16-17).

"THE FAMILY that prays together stays together" is
an expression we have heard so often, we shrug it
off without really thinking about the truth in it. After
all, everyone can give examples of families who faithfully prayed together and did *not* stay together. And
there are examples of praying families who departed
completely from God.

Why? Well, perhaps because there was not anything really "together" about the prayer time. It was
family prayer only in the sense that the bodies of the
family were present, but their minds and spirits were
totally removed.

What *is* the purpose of the family altar, anyway?

52

There are many purposes; but some are more important at one time than at others, depending on the age of the children and the family needs at any given time. Because *family* means people who grow and change, needs constantly change and shift focus also. Remember, the family altar is not merely the time period we spend praying; it extends to the total atmosphere and concern and preparation and love that go into the time slot.

The family altar should bring a family closer together. Because there are so many activities and interests that divide families, some time of joining together is important. Making God and His Word the center helps keep the family in the right focus. It can be the place where everyone from the youngest to the oldest feels free to share and open his heart with his problems and needs and know that he will be helped. Where else can we more logically expect sympathy and understanding than from our own? Comfort and encouragement weave the family fabric more tightly.

Six-year-old Susie can say, "I fell down on the playground today, and Ellen laughed. I hate her!"

But ten-year-old Bev can answer from her wide experience, "She didn't really laugh *at* you. She was just glad you weren't hurt, but she didn't know how to say that. Ellen's your friend." Who knows, tomorrow Bev may need to give herself that same advice.

The family altar is not the place to discipline in the sense of punishment. It is not the place for Mother to say severely, "Johnny was a very bad boy today, and we need to pray for him."

Instead, Mother could ask prayer for herself. "I lost my temper today over such a little thing."

Johnny, seeing her willingness to admit wrong may say, "Yeah, I got mad today, too, just 'cause someone took my eraser."

In family devotions we share what happened during the day or what we are afraid might happen tomorrow. This helps us understand one another. It is easy for adults to forget the anxieties and pressures of childhood, and especially those of the adolescent years. We brush them off with a "You think *you've* got problems! Just wait 'till you're grown!" But when there is openness in family devotions, Gwen can talk about her feeling of being on the fringe of the group at school, when she longs so desperately to belong. And Dave can talk about the hurt of always being chosen last when the guys choose sides for baseball. These things can be of special concern when parents pray together for their children.

If we are willing to stop being just people who are responsible for younger people and to show our concern for our children, they would find it easier to obey even what they think are unreasonable demands.

Sixteen-year-old Pam begged to double-date with a friend. Her father did not want her to go for an evening to an amusement park with boys he did not know and who were not Christians. He tried to explain his reasons to her through her storm of tears. Several years later, when Pam's values were more certain, she reminded her father of the incident and thanked him for standing firm. She said, "The only thing that kept me from sneaking out anyway was the way you prayed for me in devotions that night. I hated to admit it, but I knew you said no because you really cared about me."

Prayers of understanding do help to bridge the generation gap.

The family altar should give a better knowledge of the Bible. It is not supposed to be primarily a Bible-study time, of course. But we really ought to know what is in the Bible, and just reading it will help us know more. Sometimes, especially when children are little, we tend to read the same books over and over—the gospels, or parts of the Psalms, or a little dip here and there into the Old Testament. And so children grow up to be adults who have only a limited acquaintance with a small part of the Bible. Many people have no conception of the broad panorama of history unfolded in the Bible. A family altar can change this.

But do let your children grow up knowing,

Thy Word is like a garden, Lord, with flowers
   bright and fair;
And everyone who seeks may pluck a lovely cluster
   there.
Thy Word is like a deep, deep mine; and jewels rich
   and rare
Are hidden in its mighty depths for every searcher
   there.

EDWIN HODDER

Use the whole Bible in family devotions, remembering that "*all* Scripture is given by inspiration of God and is profitable" (2 Timothy 3:16, italics added). As you use it, remember the age needs and abilities and challenges in the family. See how a Bible story can supply answers to different needs. The feeding of the five thousand in John 6 applies a slightly different truth to each age. For the small child, it teaches about the boy who shared willingly. For the teenager it can be an illustration of God's use of the simplest gift we have, even when we do not think it is much. For an adult, the emphasis can be God's mighty power in action in an everyday need— feeding hungry people.

Be sure to read the Bible purposefully, entirely, and intelligently. Let everyone see the theme of God's redemption that runs, as someone has said, like a scarlet thread throughout the Bible.

The family altar is the place to practice reading the Bible aloud accurately, sincerely, and clearly, grasping the full cadence of the beauty of the language. The family altar is the place to begin a child's hunger to know what God has to say to *him* in the Bible.

The family altar should teach each member to pray out loud. If you sit in on the average prayer meeting, you would think only one or two people know how to pray. Usually a few people pray long prayers, with longer stretches of silence between the prayers. We are not usually timid about saying what we think or want at other times. But praying? Well, we just find that hard to do out loud in front of other people.

Bill Foreman was this way. He was saved when he was young, but he had never prayed in public, not even in the small prayer-meeting groups. Finally, on his sixtieth birthday, he ventured a few, faltering sentences and then broke down in tears. "My father did all the praying when I was growing up," he confessed. "This is the first time I've ever prayed out loud. My wife has even had to ask the blessing for our meals." An even worse tragedy, he admitted, was that he had never had family devotions because he could not admit to his children that he was afraid to pray in their hearing.

A family altar can help us in this. In our small group, in front of those we love and who love us, we can learn to pray simply and directly to God, who always hears. We will find out more about how to do this in chapter 6.

The family altar can strengthen personal convictions. In the Old Testament, Jewish parents were told to carry out definite ceremonies that would help them remember how they had escaped from Egypt. But they were not just to *do* them; they were supposed to know why they did them and be able to explain it to their children.

We have to do this, too, in our Christian homes. We should know the *what* of our faith—that the Bible is God's infallible, inerrant Word; that Jesus Christ is the God-man who was born of the virgin Mary, died on the cross, rose again the third day, and lives to be our Saviour; that everyone born into the world is a sinner and is completely unable to do anything to save himself; that the Holy Spirit indwells each believer and gives him the power to live a godly life; that the devil is a reality to be feared because he is powerful, but that God is greater than the devil; that Jesus Christ is coming again to reign forever.

But knowing the *what* is not enough. We must know the *why* as well and be able to explain the reasonableness of the Christian faith. We often flop miserably at this point. We are apologetic or defensive or even ashamed of our convictions. We are not absolutely sure why we believe as we do, so we have an underlying fear that we might be wrong.

Marge had this problem when she went to college. She was raised in a Christian home and a good church and knew she believed the Bible. But she had no defense against the ridicule of a religion professor who laughed at the idea of a literal interpretation of Scripture. She finally learned that her faith was reasonable and the Bible could be believed absolutely and defended when necessary.

When we are sure of our faith and confident that God's Word is "quick and powerful" (Hebrews 4:12), then we can use it and not worry when others laugh at us. Certain things *can* be accepted just because the Bible says so. But we can also have the certainty of personal conviction to back up our faith.

You see, reason always comes up against boundaries in spiritual truth. Reason can go only so far, and then it has to stop, and faith must take over. But faith in God and His Word is never a leap into the dark. Faith is always based on the absolute reliability of the Bible.

There are many ways the family altar can develop this certainty in the Bible, as we will see in chapter 6. But 1 Peter 3:15 is for parents and children equally. We all must learn to "give an answer to every man that asketh you a reason of the hope that is in you with meekness and fear."

The family altar helps answer daily problems.

This is another purpose of this time of family gathering, one we have talked about a little bit already. Let's explore it a little further.

Think about some of the Bible stories we use all the time: Queen Esther standing before the king; Nehemiah building the wall; Daniel in the lions' den. Or go back to Joseph's tempestuous life—sold by his brothers, accused by Potiphar's wife, thrown in prison, given opportunity to get even with his brothers. These are thrilling examples of courage. But they remain only examples until they are translated into everyday, "now" experience.

How do we do this? None of *us* will ever be in a lions' den. No, but some office and factory persecution of a Christian can be just as ferocious. None of *us* will ever be a queen. But we all have to take sides on issues; we are either for Christ or against Him.

If we read the story of Daniel and do not point out the underlying principle, we fail to give it the full meaning God intended it to have. God makes it clear that the whole Bible was written for everyone in all ages. Romans 15:4 says, "For whatsoever things were written aforetime"—that is, in the Old Testament—"were written for our learning, that we through patience and comfort of the scriptures might have hope."

So when Steve reads about Daniel's courage, he has to see it as more than an exciting story that actually happened to someone a long time ago. He even

needs to know more than the truth that God gives
believers courage. The point of the story must come
across to him and result in a decision: "I'm not going to let those guys talk me into getting high on
dope" or whatever temptation he is facing.

Young people today face terrific pressure to conform. So we must be sure that we help them see the
practical encouragement in Matthew 5:10-11 concerning being persecuted for righteousness' sake.

Sometimes this can be brought out from a "what
if" standpoint. What if Esther had refused to iden-
tify with the Jews? What if Joseph had yielded to
that first temptation, or Nehemiah had buckled under the sneering opposition? The consequences of
not having moral courage are sometimes worse than
the ridicule that comes with standing alone for the
right.

It develops habits of personal holiness. This purpose is a companion to the one just discussed. We
could easily become judgmental here, because we
often set standards of conduct according to our own
background, culture, training, or prejudice. And
then we feel anyone who differs from us is wrong.
In the process, we overlook inner standards and become like the Pharisees in Jesus' day, who "make
clean the outside of the cup and of the platter, but
within they are full of extortion and excess" (Matthew 23:25).

So how do we decide what is holy living? We find

out from the Word of God. Its standards apply to every age and every culture. Long ago the psalmist said, "Wherewithal shall a young man cleanse his way? by taking heed thereto according to thy word" (Psalm 119:9).

In this day of relativism and situation ethics, we have to keep going back to the solid foundation of God's Word. The Bible is not just a Book of advice; it's God's Guidebook for daily living. It gives both specific thou shalts and thou shalt nots and general principles. The Bible spells out God's basic standards. He gives them in the Ten Commandments: it is wrong to steal, to lie, to covet, to commit adultery. The New Testament warns against idolatry, witchcraft, hatred, strife, envyings, murder, drunkenness. The Lord Jesus summed God's laws as:

> Thou shalt love the Lord thy God with all thy heart, and with all thy soul, and with all thy mind, and with all thy strength: this is the first commandment. And the second is like, namely this, Thou shalt love thy neighbour as thyself (Mark 12:30-31).

Our problem comes in trying to live the way God commands. This is where the family altar helps as we work through this with our children. We have three safeguards to keep us from sin:

1. We have the authority of God's Word. We will talk about this later, in more detail, but we can

come back again and again to the cleansing feature of God's Word. We can still claim the promise of Psalm 119:11: "Thy word have I hid in mine heart, that I might not sin against thee."

2. We have the presence of the Holy Spirit. This is one of the hardest facts for us to understand. But since we never will be able to understand how the Holy Spirit helps us, let's not worry about it. Let's be glad He is there! Let Him do what He is supposed to do, which is to help us live by God's standards. What would you say to a child who did not want to learn to add two and two because he was afraid he would not understand how to do geometry? It sounds silly, doesn't it? We are like that with the Holy Spirit; we refuse His help because we do not understand the deep truths about Him. He "helpeth our infirmities" (Romans 8:26).

3. We look forward to the second coming of Jesus Christ. We have ignored this truth in teaching our children. But the Bible is very definite that the hope of Christ's return is our incentive for holy living.

> For the grace of God that bringeth salvation hath appeared to all men, teaching us that, denying ungodliness and worldly lusts, we should live soberly, righteously, and godly, in this present world; looking for that blessed hope, and the glorious ap-

pearing of the great God and our Saviour Jesus
Christ (Titus 2:11-13).

Do not avoid this subject with your children for
fear it will scare them. The Bible calls it the *blessed*
hope.

But if we are honest, most of us would give an
evasive answer to the question, Are you looking for
the Lord to return? We would say, "Yes, of course!
But—not until I'm through school, or am married,
or my children are grown."

This is because of our fear of the unknown. We
find it hard to completely believe that "eye hath not
seen, nor ear heard, neither have entered into the
heart of man, the things which God hath prepared
for them that love him" (1 Corinthians 2:9).

A story coming from World War II days in Eng-
land tells of the plans to evacuate children from
bomb-scarred London to the safety of the country.
One young boy, knowing only the bustle and com-
motion and closeness of city streets, did not want
to leave. It was not until he discovered the peace
and beauty of the country that he saw how foolish
his fears had been.

We need not be ashamed to admit that we are
afraid of the unknown. But when we arrive in
heaven, we will see how foolish the fears were. Use
the family altar to build in your children (and yourself, if you need it) the excitement of anticipating

Christ's return. It is one of the chief incentives to holy living.

Then the family altar helps us worship God because it brings us into close touch with Him. We have to avoid two extremes in teaching our children about God. One is to picture Him as stern and remote, waiting to pounce on every little mistake. Some people see God as Someone to fear, Someone who will deprive us of something we need or desire. Those who think this have never known the God who "so loved the world, that he gave his only begotten Son" (John 3:16).

The other extreme to avoid is the too-familiar, buddy-buddy attitude which views God as a kindly, nodding Grandfather who dismisses sin with a light slap on the wrist. This is the view of those who see Him only as a God of love and do not recognize that above all He is holy.

In your family altar and in all your conversations, give your children a true picture of God. He is indeed our heavenly Father, who wants us to come to Him gladly for everything we need. His invitation in Hebrews 4:16 to "come boldly unto the throne of grace, that we may obtain mercy, and find grace to help in time of need" includes Andy's lost bike and Susan's broken engagement and Grandma's huge hospital bill.

But 2 Corinthians 5:10 is just as true, "We must

all appear before the judgment seat of Christ." Help your children learn that God does not excuse sin in His children. We *never* lose our salvation, but we will lose out on rewards in heaven if we do not live as we should now.

Do you think this is hard for children to understand? Not really—because it happens in family life sometimes. Alison was having so much fun playing with Kathy she pretended not to hear her older sister calling her name over and over again. When she finally went home, she found that Uncle Bob had dropped in for an unexpected visit and had taken the other children to the zoo. She missed out because of what really was a lie—pretending not to hear.

You see, the Lord Jesus has to be more than the "unseen Guest at every meal" in our homes. The family altar should give Him the key to every door and open an entrance to every room.

Your family is *God's* family; He wants it to succeed. He will give wisdom and understanding and increase your love for each other.

Happy the home when God is there, and love fills
every breast;
When one their wish, and one their prayer, and one
their heavenly rest.
Happy the home where Jesus' Name is sweet to every
ear;

Where children early lisp His fame, and parents hold
Him dear.

Happy the home where prayer is heard, and praise is
wont to rise;

Where parents love the sacred Word, and all its wisdom prize.

CARL J. P. SPITTA
TRANS. SARAH B. FINDLATER

5

Getting It Ready

I rejoice at thy word, as one that findeth great spoil. . . . My lips shall utter praise, when thou hast taught me thy statutes (Psalm 119:162, 171).

SEVEN-YEAR-OLD Julie sat surrounded by brightly colored wrapping paper and gay ribbons she had pulled off her packages. She looked around and sighed. "The trouble with Christmas is, you look forward to it for *so* long, and then it's over right away."

Most of us can share Julie's feelings of anticipation. We have all looked forward to a fun time or an out-of-the-ordinary event, and we know the feeling of excitement.

But you are probably asking how this can *possibly* apply to family devotions, because you do not remember them being exciting at all as you grew up. Your memories are of a deadly boring time, with one of your parents reading a long, hard-to-under-

68

stand chapter and the other parent praying an endless prayer.

But you see, that is *not* family worship, nor is it *family* worship, nor is it family *worship*. You can change that image in your home and make the family altar an enjoyable, looked-forward-to habit that puts zest into each day. It all depends on what you put into it.

First, develop the same anticipation you have for some fun, exciting event, the kind of eagerness children have for Christmas. Do not let anybody tell you it is wrong to have a good time when you read the Bible; do not let your children grow up with that idea!

The Bible has a lot to say about happy anticipation. It says:

"Rejoice"—why?

"For the coming of the Lord draweth nigh" (James 5:8).

"Rejoice and be exceeding glad"—why?

"For great is your reward in heaven" (Matthew 5:12).

"Rejoice greatly"—why?

"Thy King cometh unto thee" (Zechariah 9:9).

"Rejoice"—when?

"Evermore" (1 Thessalonians 5:16).

This attitude of anticipation carries into all our activities. It can make us see the dancing of lights reflected in a puddle of water instead of seeing the mud we might step in. And it can make us enjoy family devotions rather than having them only because we think God will be angry at us if we do not read the Bible every day. We know that the principle of reaping what we sow applies to people who do wicked things. But it also can mean that the sullenness and grumpiness we show are reflected in the faces of those around us. And our children will get from us either an "Oh, boy! It's time for devotions!" or an "I suppose we've got to read the *Bible* again!"

Humans seem to have the concept that the harder something is, the better it must be. Or, the more expensive it is, the more valuable. This may be true in some areas, but it is not an infallible guide for spiritual truths. Some people are unable to accept the free gift of salvation simply because it *is* free, and they prefer to earn it.

And some never accept Christ, because they think Christianity is a joyless religion. Sadly, even some Christians think it is a duty, a burden they have to bear while being cheated out of the pleasures non-Christians enjoy. Paul exclaimed, "Rejoice in the Lord alway: and again I say, Rejoice!" (Philippians 4:4). Let's develop this attitude of rejoicing and anticipation, because we cannot act happy unless we are.

If you have been having family devotions—grimly—and no one has been enjoying them, make a fresh start. Infect your children with the joyous exclamation of the psalmist: "Open thou mine eyes, that I may behold wondrous things out of thy law" (Psalm 119:18).

You will probably need a lot of preparation. Now, it is true that sometimes exciting things happen without any planning. Something unexpected turns up; a friend drops in to visit; a letter brings surprising news and changes your plans. But this is the unusual. After all, even the surprise birthday party has *some* planning behind it.

So family worship requires careful preparation to make it the vital part of life we would like it to be. How do we do it?

First, have that expectant attitude we have already spoken of. Let the Word of God grip *you*. Let it "dwell in you richly in all wisdom" (Colossians 3:16). Find in it the wisdom and strength *you* need. When you do, you'll be eager for your children to have this same joy in God.

Then talk over the project with the whole family. Be frank about the hindrances that could interfere, the age differences you have, the interruptions that might come which could discourage you. Let each one tell what he wants to get out of family devotions and what he wants to include.

Second, choose materials and subjects that suit your children's ages, capabilities, levels of understanding, and needs. This will be one of the hardest parts of the preparation. The next several chapters will give you ideas.

Third, decide when to have your worship time. You probably will not have much leeway here, because family schedules usually determine this, and most of us have pretty tight schedules. You will want to pick the time the father is usually home, which generally means that right after dinner in the evening is the best time. But you do not have to have your devotions then just because your neighbors do or you did that in your home when you were growing up. Maybe for your family it will work better to have the family altar later, after the dishes and homework are done or you have come back from some necessary evening activity or Bruce is home from basketball practice. Sometimes you will have to settle the baby in bed first.

Perhaps you are not able to have family devotions every day but can manage only three days a week or every other day or weekends. It is good to have family altar every day, but do not let not having it every day keep you from having it at all. Do what is best to bring your family before God on some kind of a regular basis.

What should you do when a meeting or activity interferes? Generally we let the family altar take a back seat to other activities. Do not let this happen!

Plan around the family time. Just be sure that what does take precedence over the family altar really *is* more important. Prayer meeting at church, especially if the whole family can go, can take the place of the family time for an evening. And, by the way, make this decision a family affair, and let everyone express an opinion.

Decide also how much time you will spend. You cannot be rigid about this. Some nights you may have only ten minutes; another time an hour will go by before you stop. You don't believe it? Well, try some of the ideas in the next several chapters. If you include even the youngest children in the devotional period, then it will, of course, be briefer than if the children are all older. Just keep in mind that you are building a habit of learning from God and worshiping Him, and you do not want to turn anyone off. If you prolong family devotions to the point where you battle to keep the children quiet, you will defeat your purpose. It is much better to stop while everyone's interest is high, so that anticipation can build for the next time. As the children grow, the time span will automatically lengthen.

I would suggest being brief on evenings when you have to attend necessary meetings. You can pare the devotion time to the bone with one person praying briefly and everyone joining to repeat one Bible verse from memory. Or have devotions during the dinner hour in a conversational way. You can think of many ways to do this, and it will keep the daily habit line unbroken.

Fourth, let the Bible come alive for the family. You may have to *make* it so at first, while you are getting started, but after a while your enthusiasm will be contagious. Getting your family into the Word will take work by you, since as parents God gave you the responsibility for the family altar. But you can help your children grow with you by helping in the preparation.

Let's say your home has a five-year-old, eight-year-old twins, a fifteen-year-old, and a grandparent. Your family devotions have been hit and miss, a haphazard affair which often ends in scoldings and tears. Grandpa wonders—out loud and often—why you do not make the twins pay attention. The five-year-old sits still only when he can play with toys—noisily; and the fifteen-year-old is frankly bored. And you, in your turn, read the Bible passage as fast as possible to get through before it all explodes.

There is not an easy solution to this situation or the many other equally sticky ones. There are no magic formulas that will bring everyone to the edge of their seats, immediately eager to read the Bible. But if you are really concerned that you and your children have a family time together with God, you can take the steps that will help you be successful.

It will take work, and you will have to have the

whole family working with you. Talk your problem over with the children—yes, even the squirmy beginner. Open your heart to them and ask for their suggestions. Find what part of the Bible they like best; you might find it is not the part they know best.

If they do not have any ideas, start reading the gospel of Mark. It is brief and full of action. It has vivid pictures: John the Baptist in the desert; the paralyzed man carried by his friends; the storm on the sea. Fascinating studies will open to you, to all of you. The twins can ask some questions to find out what John actually ate. Was it *really* grasshoppers? Like ours? How could the men in chapter 2 take the roof off the house? What were the houses like, anyway? Ask the five-year-old to draw a picture of the boat on the water, with lightning flashing and dark, black clouds. He can do this while the rest of you are finding what is in the story for you.

The familiar story of John the Baptist in chapter 6 has a dimension your fifteen-year-old daughter may not have discovered. The implications of Herod's family life make for sobering discussion. How could a mother make such an evil, gory request? How could a daughter go along with it? Are there homes like that today? What would I do if my home were like that? Are there times when I have to refuse to do something that is wrong? You may not always get a verbal response, but you will start some serious thinking.

If you are planning to read aloud through a book of the Bible, assign parts of it in advance to different family members so they will have a chance to practice and work out ideas to make it interesting to the rest of you.

Help your children grow; stretch their minds and talents and creativity. But at the same time, do not expect more than they can really do. This means you will have to know what they are capable of at different age levels. Maybe you have been scolding Kevin for not sitting still for a half-hour quiet time, when his three-year-old engine just does not work that way yet.

Children are all different and do not react the way books say they should at the exact time and to the exact degree. But there are basic age characteristics that are generally true of preschoolers, juniors, and adolescents. It is wise to know and use them in building family devotions.

As you look at the next paragraphs, remember that they are only general descriptions of age groups. Much more could be said about each of the age levels, but there is enough here to apply to your children and remind you not to expect seven-year-old Sally to pay the same attention seventeen-year-old Donna will.

We will start with the two- and three-year-olds, because children younger than that do better if they have a quiet time with Mother and/or Dad all alone.

NURSERY—TWOS AND THREES

PHYSICALLY, MENTALLY, AND SOCIALLY

They tire easily and have a short attention span; are restless and do not sit still long; are prone to temper tantrums; usually play alone; are imitators; do not share easily; "read" pictures by telling what they see in them; like repetition—of words, sounds, stories; are learning to sing; should be asked questions to stimulate thinking; are taught best in brief moments with love and patience.

TEACHING AT THE FAMILY ALTAR

God loves him; God made the world; God takes care of him; Jesus is his Friend; the Bible is God's Book and tells about God; he should obey his parents; church is a place to learn about God.

BEGINNER—FOURS AND FIVES

PHYSICALLY, MENTALLY, AND SOCIALLY

They are growing rapidly; have much energy; need alternate periods of activity and quiet; learn through their senses (they just *have* to touch!); have a limited sense of time; forget easily; are friendly but easily afraid; are curious and literal-minded; constantly talk; want to know why; are learning to print; enjoy stories; need opportunity to practice Bible truths such as sharing.

TEACHING AT THE FAMILY ALTAR

God loves him; God sent Jesus to die for sin; Jesus died for him and is always with him; Jesus is in heaven; Jesus will help him obey his parents; the Bible is God's Word; the Bible tells us what God wants us to do; not obeying parents is wrong; God wants him to be kind and to share; church is a special place where he learns about God.

PRIMARY—SIX, SEVEN, AND EIGHT

PHYSICALLY, MENTALLY, AND SOCIALLY

Sixes are sometimes closer to beginners and eights closer to juniors, so we make allowances for behavior at both ends of the primary age. But these three years do share similar needs, behavior patterns, contrariness, and sweetness. They are curious and impatient; need activity; are literal-minded but have an active imagination; believe what they are told; are learning to read; need help in discovering their abilities; live in the present, and tomorrow is a long way off; know they *should* behave but have trouble doing it always; are developing a concern for others; need calmness and order; must have concrete learning situations.

TEACHING AT THE FAMILY ALTAR

God is good and holy and loves all people; God has power to help him; God is the Creator who loves him; Jesus is God's Son; Jesus came to earth as a Baby; He died and rose again and is now in heaven; Jesus can help him choose to do right instead of wrong; the Bible is God's Book and tells about Him; the Bible stories are true (they should be told exactly as they are, without imaginative material added); God gave him parents to take care of him; he must be kind to others; he should pray for other people and tell them about Jesus; church is more than a building—it is the people in it; Satan tries to make people sin; he needs to accept Jesus as his Saviour; if he does he will be with Jesus in heaven forever.

JUNIORS—NINE, TEN, AND ELEVEN

PHYSICALLY, MENTALLY, AND SOCIALLY

Age characteristics are blurred here, as with the primaries. Some nine-year-olds are close to eights in actions and responses; some elevens have almost stepped over into adolescence. But in general, they are alike. Several strong words describe them: *doer, discoverer, loud, active, independent, noisy, competitive.* They have a good memory; like to reason and want facts; love hobbies; like to collect; are strongly influenced by the group; have a strong sense of justice; insist on fair play from parents and teachers; like to make things; have a good attention span; are hero worshipers without always choosing the best examples to copy; can understand historical information; like to find where things are; do not easily apply truth to life situations; like action stories; read well if they enjoy reading.

TEACHING AT THE FAMILY ALTAR

God is all-wise and all-powerful and is everywhere at the same time; He hates sin; He takes care of His people; He has a purpose for everyone's life; Jesus died and rose again and lives in heaven; Jesus was born of a virgin; He was sinless; Jesus is coming again; the Bible tells about the history of the world; the Bible is God's Word and has no mistakes; he should obey God's Word and memorize it; he should obey his parents and be loyal to them; he should forgive others and be kind to others; he should be unselfish; God wants him to tell others about Jesus; Satan is a powerful ruler who does not want people to love God; Satan will be punished by God forever; the Church is people who love God and the Lord Jesus; a church is a place to serve God by helping others; one way he can serve God is by sharing his money for the church to use.

ADOLESCENTS—TWELVE TO SEVENTEEN

I am not lumping all teenagers together—far from it! These years are the most impossible to say, "They're all like this" or "They all think and act this way," because it is not so. Adolescents of the same age, the same grade in school, the same family, can be poles apart in appearance, actions, beliefs, and responses. *Except,* they are all in a time of growth and transition and are reaching out, trying to find themselves and understand life. They all need depths of love, guidance, sympathy, understanding, and stability, to bring them through the struggles to belong and the group pressure to conform. They need to know they can trust God; that Jesus will never fail them; that He is a Person who can be more real to them than their closest friend; that the Bible is absolutely reliable and shows them God's picture of a Christian; that *they* can fit that picture by letting the Holy Spirit help them.

Do not let these characteristics remain general to you. See where they fit your family. Billy is your beginner. Have you been insisting that he sit still for a twenty-minute family worship?

Janie is your teenager, with eager questions about life. But you use only simple songs and bits of Bible stories to keep the younger children's interest. Or you use stories like Jacob's and Esau's rivalry for heavy-handed lectures on behavior. In the process you turn your children against the idea of a family altar.

Worst of all, you turn them from God and His tender, loving concern for them and give them a dislike for the Book that can revolutionize their lives. Do not do it! Make the family altar a delight to your family.

Fifth, plan the mechanics of family devotion. Decide where you will sit (not that you will have to be in the same place every time), who will lead (and not always Dad), what to do when you are interrupted. It is up to you whether you want to stay at the cluttered dinner table, which can give a comfortable, at-home feeling, or move to the living room or family room or a bedroom. The place is only important as it contributes to family closeness and keeps you free from distractions.

One of the biggest distractions is the telephone, for when it rings—and it *always* does during devotions—you have to answer. Decide beforehand who will answer—and do let one of the younger children feel the importance of this job now and then—and simply say, "We're having family devotions. May we call you back?" Most callers will not be offended; and it does give a testimony—not to them, about how holy your family is, but to your children, about how important you think your time with God is.

Then sometimes neighbor children come to play, especially in summer. This interruption will be minimal if your children let their friends know they cannot play for a while after dinner. But sometimes the children forget or come anyway and sit outside waiting. *Your* children know their friends are there and become impatient.

Perhaps you will want to invite the neighbor children in. If they are not from Christian families and

what you do is interesting, they may say at home,
"Why can't we have fun reading the Bible the way
Sally and Jimmy do?" And so your home will reach
out in a way you did not expect when you planned
your family altar.

You will want to be careful about this, though,
for several reasons. Including other children can
limit what you do with your own family. Your children might not open up as freely to you in front of
their friends. If this is the case, you will have to
work out some other solution and not lose this valuable family time.

Then, too, if the neighbors are not Christians, they
might object to their children being exposed to your
odd beliefs. Of course, you have a right to witness
for Christ, and the neighbor children have a right
to hear; but not if their parents object. Try talking
to the neighbors over the back fence or while you
are sharing a cup of coffee, and explain what you
do—"We have such a good time talking about all the
things God does for us. Do you mind if Paul and
Jeff join us?" If the parents agree, you could invite
them, too. It could mean a step to salvation, if they
are not believers. If they are, sharing your family
time could make them enthusiastic to have their own
family altar.

If your neighbors want no part of what you do,
do not insist. But do not be huffy and cut them off,
either. Find other ways to be neighborly, and wait

for the right time for God to work through you. Draw your children into this with you. Are you praying as a family for the lost in Africa or India? Why not make the people next door your special family project?

What do you do with a crying child? First of all, comfort him, regardless of his age or the reason for the tears. Even though you remember the age characteristics and plan your devotions accordingly, a child's nervous system is temperamental, and tears come very easily. It is better to put a very young child to bed early, with a song and a good-night prayer as his quiet time. An older young child can be all ready for bed and enjoy a brief part of the time with the whole family before going to bed. This will not be an interruption if the rest of the family sings or carries on some other group activity while Mother and/or Dad say good night to the littler ones.

What you are trying to do is make your family time so enjoyable that the younger children can hardly wait until they can share it all. In the meantime, the older children are aware of their status as responsible family members who share in the planning as well as the doing.

But what do you do when you have guests? If they are Christians and can share your Bible and prayer time, there is no problem. But even so, remember this is *your family* time with God, and you are not doing it primarily for the visitors.

If guests will be sharing with you, tell the family about it in advance. Maybe it is the night your nine-year-old is going to read the Scripture, and he will be scared or embarrassed to do it in front of extra people. Let him have special practice with you alone, and help him read it smoothly. Or adjust the schedule if he really does not want to take his turn. Keep the devotions as natural as possible, or you will end up trying to impress your company.

If your guests are not believers, explain what you do and give them the option of either sharing with you or waiting in another room—without embarrassment. *Do not* use this time as an opportunity to witness to them of their need of Christ. If they do share with you, and your enthusiasm brings them to God, wonderful! But do not let that be the motive of your devotions. Remember again that this is family devotions for family growth. Let God be the One to use your family altar to win someone to Christ.

This situation is especially touchy if the guests are unsaved family members—grandparents, perhaps, or aunts or uncles who are completely out of sympathy with your family goals. Again, while you must be gentle and loving, your family time must be guarded. Do not let your attitude condemn them or make you seem holier than they are because you read the Bible. Be gracious. But remember that you are at home, and you have the responsibility for the day's activities.

It is different if you are the guests, and your hosts are uncomfortable if anyone even mentions God. You can change your usual habits. If you are used to automatically reaching for your Bible when dessert is finished, do not insist on doing it in Uncle Ed's house if he does not want you to. Remember Jesus' words to His disciples in Matthew 10? "Be ye . . . wise as serpents, and harmless as doves" (v. 16).

You want to be wise and gentle at the same time, so you will try new ways to have family worship. You can go for a walk after supper, even on a cold night, and talk about the wonder of God's creation as you watch the stars come out. Congregate for a brief family time in one of the bedrooms you are using. Write out a Bible verse, and let everyone learn it on his own during the day. This is a great time to be creative and come up with new ideas you can use in family worship when you get back home.

After all, there is no one right way to have a family altar. The only requirement is that you all come to God, remembering His promise in Jeremiah 33: 3: "Call unto me, and I will answer thee, and shew thee great and mighty things, which thou knowest not." This promise is just as true for you and me now as it was for the prophet in his time. We just have to believe it!

6

Putting Something into It

When I was a child, I spake as a child, I understood
as a child, I thought as a child: but when I became
a man, I put away childish things. For now we see
through a glass, darkly; but then face to face: now
I know in part; but then shall I know even as also
I am known (1 Corinthians 13:11-12).

YEAR-OLD JEFF is the darling of the family, with his
wide grin and the chubby hands that reach out so
appealingly and the funny sounds he makes when he
tries to talk.

But if he has these same babyish features four
years later, he is a tragic case for his heartbroken
parents.

First Corinthians 3 reminds us that Christians do
not always grow as they should. This is because
they do not receive nourishment at the right time to
help them put away spiritually childish things. The
family devotional time, carried out month by month

and year by year, can help parents and children grow stronger and taller and more surefooted in their Christian faith. Paul puts the same idea this way in Ephesians 4:13-14, where he talks about our coming to "the knowledge of the Son of God, unto a perfect man, unto the measure of the stature of the fulness of Christ: That we henceforth be no more children, tossed to and fro, and carried about with every wind of doctrine."

What can we use in family devotions that will help us mature as God expects? First of all, the Bible is the only reliable source for anything we know about God or other aspects of our Christian faith. Whatever we know about angels, Satan, sin, the future, heaven, or hell comes from the Bible. Of course, encyclopedias and literature discuss these subjects; but unless the information is based on the Bible, it is either inaccurate or pure imagination.

But the Bible answers all the questions we ask: who we are; why we are here; where we are going. The Bible tells us how to get along with other people; it explains history. The Bible is God's revelation of Himself.

Even though we parents know all this, our children will not know we do unless we use the Bible at home. And the place it should especially be used is in the family altar. This does not mean we cannot use other books and materials. But everything else should flow out of or back to Bible truth.

How we use the Bible depends primarily on the individual family situation. What works for a couple with no children will not do at all for a family with young children. And what might work one year, might not another. So flexibility and adaptability are vital.

Here are suggestions that will give you ideas of your own. They will help no matter what setup you are in—whether you have never had a family altar; you have had one, and it flopped, so you are afraid to try again; or you have one and it is going great, but you are always looking for new ideas.

When You Use the Bible

1. *Use the Bible itself.* Some families have a special Bible to use in family devotions, the large kind that has a place for family records. In some families, each person has a different translation so they can compare readings. Do use the King James Version along with others, even when you have small children who might be lost by some of the words. The beauty and majesty of the English language is often lost in a newer translation and certainly in a paraphrase. We also lose many expressions that have found their way into literature from the King James Version. We cheat children of much richness if we use only modern translations. But whatever translation you use, be sure to actually read from the Bible.

What about using a Bible storybook instead of the actual text of Scripture? No, not *instead* of. It is good to use a Bible storybook as a supplement for small children, but do not let it take the place of the Bible text. Even if one of the fine paraphrases is used, always have it as an aid to understanding and not as a replacement for a translation.

2. *Use the whole Bible.* Many years ago, Dr. James M. Gray, a former president of Moody Bible Institute, discovered a secret that revolutionized his life. He found that the best way to know the Bible was to read it, and to read it over and over again.

How can we do this in family devotions? By choosing a book of the Bible and reading through it, and then reading another and another. If it is not too long, a whole chapter can be read at one time. If it is, divide it; but be careful to divide it logically and not end your reading in the middle of a thought.

Of course, not every book will be equally usable for family devotions. It is true that all Scripture is God-breathed and all of it is true and all of it is important. But it is not all equally applicable to every situation. The books of Numbers and Leviticus are not as important to the daily life of an eight-year-old as is the command of Ephesians 4:32. Later, when the eight-year-old is fourteen, a research study of the tabernacle or the Levitical system of sacrifice could be fascinating.

But many books of the Bible can be read through

chapter by chapter. Try Ruth or Jonah or Mark or James. Acts is full of exciting events along with deep doctrinal truths children can begin to learn at home, with you as their teacher. Do not neglect the Old Testament books. Paul told Timothy that it was the holy Scriptures which made him wise to salvation. Obviously he was talking about the Old Testament, since the New Testament books were just then being written.

3. *Read the Bible carefully.* In some family devotion setups, only the father reads, or the mother if he is not there, with everyone else listening—supposedly. But it is so easy to let our attention wander when we are just hearing words. We do it, so we can be sure our children have the same problem; and that is one reason why family devotions come across as boring and unimportant and unrelated to life.

There are many ways to vary your routine. One is to let everyone have a turn reading the whole passage, let everyone read a verse around, or let the children read one night and the parents another. Or instead of reading Scripture, everyone can join in to repeat a passage by heart.

What about beginning readers? Should Patty, who is just learning to read, stumble through the verse when her turn comes? She does not have to stumble through it. She can be told in advance which verses she will have and can practice them. Of course, you could give her verses without any hard words; but how much better to learn to read the hard ones along with the easy ones.

In fact, the family altar is a good place for everyone to practice reading the Bible, parents as well as children. We have all heard ministers in the pulpit read Scripture carelessly, without paying attention to punctuation and often mispronouncing words and hard names. If we really believe this is *God's* Word, we can show our respect by careful, accurate, clear reading. This is part of what it means to handle Scripture reverently.

Try having at least one copy of a large-print Bible in your home. Young, just-learning-to-read children and elderly members of the family read more easily if they can see the words clearly.

Do not ever ignore the Bible or think it is too difficult to understand or, worse still, think it does not apply to our generation. The Bible is timeless; it has something for people in every age. God has promised that His Word will do what He wants it to (Isaiah 55:11); we can trust Him to use it in our lives and our children's.

You can help your children value the Bible for themselves if you find ways to make it come alive for them.

4. *Use helps in understanding the Bible.* The ways suggested here are only springboards from which you can take off with your own creative ideas. Some of these will work for you, and some will not. Re-

member, you are not having a family altar just to raise your hand when the minister asks or just to say you read the Bible. You want everyone in the family to *hear* the Word and *remember* it and put it into practice. Knowing Bible facts is important—that Peter had a vision on the housetop (Acts 10). But we need as well the Bible truth that Peter objected to God's command, "Rise, Peter; kill, and eat," because it was against his Jewish heritage. He did not see the truth God was showing him, that salvation is for all men. We need to help our children go beyond Bible facts, important as they are, to Bible truths. But first of all, facts should be learned, and there are many ways to teach them.

First, find out what is actually in the Bible. What does a book say? One way to discover this is to chart the book on a large piece of poster board. The book of Acts lends itself well to this, and the action becomes clearer if we are able to see the scope of the book at a glance. For example:

Author—Luke, by the Holy Spirit

29-30 A.D.	Key verse: Acts 1:8	A.D. 60-62
Peter, James, Stephen witness		Paul's missionary journeys
Chapter: 1 — 7	8 — 12	13 — 28
Jerusalem	Judea / Samaria	Uttermost parts of the world
Church started	Church scattered	Church growing

You can do this chart in several ways. You may want to chart the whole book before you begin to read, so you can follow the action. But it is more fun to put only the main dividing line across the poster board, and then let everyone add to the chart as you make discoveries together. Of course, even when you have this much of the book on paper, there is a lot more to know about the *message* of the book. But at least you have the main structure down in a manageable form, and you can see how it all fits together.

This business of seeing relationships in Scripture is very important. A lot of people do not know that the Bible is not sixty-six separate books but sixty-six books that make one Book with one message, God's revelation of Himself and His purpose for the world. All the books fit together.

Think about Exodus, with its rules about priests and sacrifices. Why were those regulations given? You may be able to understand that the Israelites needed them, but why should *we* know about them? The book of Hebrews gives the answer as it teaches about Christ, who is our High Priest and our Sacrifice. Hebrews and Exodus—they explain each other.

And of course, if we did not have Genesis, we would not know why the Israelites had to leave Egypt, so those two books belong together. These are discoveries you and your children can make together in your family altar time. Why, your children may never have realized that the New Testament letters of Galatians and Ephesians and Colossians and Philippians came out of Paul's experiences in the book of Acts. A whole new world of discovering exciting facts about the Bible can open to them.

Help them gather new insights into the value of the Bible by finding out how we got the Bible. Where did it come from? Do not do this by having Mother or Dad reading from a history book but by everyone having assignments to do their own investigating. Find information in books like Jack Finegan's *Light from the Ancient Past* (Princeton: Princeton U., 1969) or Neil Lightfoot's *How We Got the Bible* (Grand Rapids: Baker, 1962) or F. F. Bruce's *The Books and the Parchment*s, rev. ed. (Westwood, N.J.: Revell, 1953). See if these are in your church library or on the pastor's bookshelves or in the public library. You can also look in encyclopedias for some basic information such as when people first began to write.

Try not to make these into assignments that have to be done like homework; let them grow out of your Bible reading.

Go back to Acts again to chapter 7, which describes Moses as being "learned in all the wisdom of Egypt." This takes you back to Exodus, of course, and you know already that Moses was raised as a prince in the king's house. But how smart were the Egyptians then? And just when was that? When *did* Moses live? This opens another fascinating study, as you and your children begin to dovetail secular and biblical history. You may find that your children have never thought of Bible history, geography, and people as really *belonging* anywhere.

You will want your children to know in what languages the Bible was originally written, and this will lead into the intensely interesting story of how the Bible came to us through many manuscripts and copies and translations. Knowing this has double value: it will be interesting to them while they are making these discoveries, but invaluable to them in high school and college years when someone scoffs, "How can you believe the Bible! You think Moses wrote the first five books—why, he didn't even know how to write!" And your children's faith will remain unshaken as they pull out of the treasury of their minds the information you helped them store away during your family devotions.

Use Bible games to teach Bible facts. If you cannot find any you like, then make up your own. Part of assimilating the Bible is knowing people and their relationships—Abraham, Sarah, Hagar, Esau, Nehemiah, Jeremiah and Baruch, Job, Saul and Jonathan, Paul, Barnabas, Lydia, Dorcas.

Help your children learn how to use a concordance, and give them practice finding verses. Give them a Bible dictionary that will explain words. Some are written particularly for children to give extra facts about Bible people, history, geography, and customs.

Use lots of maps! You will need them especially when reading the Old Testament books to know where Abraham was when he answered God's call, or what spot it was that Jacob saw the ladder that reached to heaven (and *that* is a good place to stop and sing the chorus, "We Are Climbing Jacob's Ladder"). You will use the map a lot when you follow the journey of the Israelites or move with the Lord Jesus around the land of Palestine or travel with Paul on his missionary journeys.

You do not always need to have a ready-made map. Let the children draw an outline map of Egypt and Palestine large enough to write place names and events on it or to draw stick figures to illustrate the Bible stories. Find out from an atlas something about the land—its climate, how much it rains, how high was the mountain that Moses climbed when he received the Ten Commandments. These are things your primary and junior and older children can do.

But do not forget the wiggly four- and five-year-olds who need some action. All of you can act out the Bible stories. Let the older children write the scripts if you want to be fancy, and direct the plays, while the younger ones act the parts. Naaman and the slave girl in 2 Kings 5, the good Samaritan in Luke 10, and the story of the lost coin in Luke 15 come alive in this way.

You can use this method to teach Bible fact and Bible truth. You know how light reflecting on a diamond flashes many-colored sparks. Scripture truths also sparkle with various shades of meaning. Help your children see this in the story in 2 Kings 5. To appreciate the courage of the little girl in speaking to her master of the power of her God, find out something about the life of a slave. What could have happened to her if Naaman had *not* been healed? After you have acted out the biblical story, put it in a modern setting. Have the children work through an original story illustrating the theme of being true to Christ in a hard situation. The result may give you a new insight to your children's thinking on a problem that perhaps you are unaware of.

With these ideas to start you off, you will come up with many more that just suit your family. Watch out though—you will have those neighbor children begging to join you!

When You Pray

Prayer is a second essential in family worship. We have talked already about how important family devotions can be in teaching children to pray. Do not discourage them by your long, beautifully worded prayers. Real prayer is not the words we say but the condition of our heart before God.

Remember the principle we use when we train children in other ways. At meals we give small amounts of food, cut into small pieces. We do not expect children to have polished manners; we even let them use their fingers when they first begin to feed themselves.

The storybooks we give them are colorful, with only a few words on a page. Children's first steps are faltering, and we catch them with delight and help them try again.

Let's do this as we teach them to pray. Start with a few words and a single idea. Young children are self-centered and relate God to themselves, so their first prayers are, "Help me." Gradually we will use family prayer time to help put away the "childish things" and learn to pray for others and then to thank God and praise Him. Of course, none of us ever leaves the place where, as the spiritual says, we are "standing in the need of prayer."

Praying for specific things will keep us from rambling. Note how definite the Lord's prayer is in Matthew 6: "Thy will be done"; "give us . . . our daily bread"; "forgive us our debts"; "lead us not into temptation"; "deliver us from evil."

Do not be guilty of lazily praying for "the missionaries around the world." Pray for "Jim Green as he operates on patients so he'll have a steady hand." Or pray for "Five-year-old Mike so he won't fall off the burro while he's riding up the steep mountain trail."

Then be flexible in the way you pray. Sometimes

assign the requests—ask Sue to pray that Grandma will be patient as she tries to get used to her hearing aid. Another time pray around the group by turn. Try reading a short Psalm in unison as a prayer. Sometimes the prayers can be conversational, each one praying just one sentence.

Try kneeling or standing; or have everyone hold hands, while each prays silently. Ask someone to look up verses in the Bible that show different postures of prayer and try each of them—including lying face down! Do not do this *just* to be different, because you might forget the purpose of your praying. Use these methods only if they help make praying more important to you.

If you are going to pray for missionaries and for each other, you will have to find out specific needs. You could have a prayer suggestion box. In the family room or basement, put up a blackboard on which to jot down needs. Keep a notebook of requests, recording the date you began praying and the date the request was answered. After all, prayer is not just asking; it is also seeing answers to the asking.

One family bought a bright red notebook and pasted a picture of a missionary family on one page. On the opposite page, they wrote two prayer needs that five-year-old Amy could remember. One was, "Jesus, keep the mosquitoes from biting Patty Lou, so she won't get sick"; and the other, "Jesus, help

Billy find the toy he lost when he packed." They put
the date of the request in blue and the answer in red.

But how can Amy's parents explain when she
asks, "Why didn't God help Billy find his toy? He
needs it so he won't get lonesome in Africa." Every
child—and even parents sometimes—ask the question, Why didn't God answer my prayer? What we
mean is, Why didn't He answer the way I wanted
Him to?

In this case Mother said, "Billy left it behind in
the motel, and nobody knew who it belonged to. But
God can use you to help answer if you share one of
your toys with Billy."

Even while your children are young, help them
face honestly the fact that God does answer prayer
always; but He does not always answer the way we
want Him to, and when He doesn't, His answer ulti-
mately is the right one. This is not an easy truth to
learn, so look for ways outside the actual family altar
time to reenforce it in your family's experience. Try
using this poem in family discussion, and let everyone react to it.

I asked God for strength, that I might achieve;
I was made weak, that I might learn to obey.

I asked for health, that I might do greater things;
I was given infirmity, that I might do better things.

I asked for riches, that I might be happy;
I was given poverty that I might be wise.

I asked for power, that I might have the praise of
    men;
I was given weakness, that I might feel the need
    of God.

I asked for all things, that I might enjoy all things;
I received nothing I had asked for but everything I
    had hoped for.

My prayers were answered.

AUTHOR UNKNOWN

Accepting God's answers and waiting for Him
to work is one of the most difficult things we impatient humans must learn. As parents we must re-
peatedly say things like, "Honey, I don't know why
God let Mary Ann fall off her bike in front of the
car. But we can trust Him, because He loves her
more than we do."

Family prayer time can be an ointment that
smoothes relationships and helps our family live har-
moniously. We do not dare pray sanctimoniously in
the hearing of those to whom we have just said
harsh, bitter words.

This does not mean a father cannot pray after
punishing a child—in fact, that is one of the best
times *to* pray with the child. But Father must first
pray for himself, asking God for love, patience, understanding, concern.

Grandpa Taylor came to live with the Pattersons
and drove his daughter to distraction as he followed

her around the house giving advice, comparing the children unfavorably, and complaining about her cooking. Finally one evening in family devotions, she prayed impulsively, "Thank You, God, for letting us have Grandpa share our home," and then discovered she really *was* thankful. But she found, too, that Grandpa's attitude changed. He had been so afraid he was an unwanted burden that he had not known how to act and so was critical and defensive.

Just how personal should we be in family praying? No one can make a general rule about this. Some needs are too personal to share at first in front of a teasing brother or a critical sister. In such a case, try a prayer-partner system, each sharing a need with only the family member with whom he feels most at ease.

Anne was so conscious of her acne she was defensive and snappish and usually ended each day in tears of self-pity. Finally her mother offered to pray with her about her skin condition. In their conversations, Anne gradually came to understand that God already knew all about her problem and how real it was to her. The next step was realizing that God had made her that way. Then came the knowledge that since she had already trusted Him with her eternal salvation, she could also trust Him to take care of her face. Eventually she gained enough poise to share her need with the whole family and found even the teasing younger brother understanding. "I've got a problem too," he said. "Whenever I have to do something on the blackboard, the back of my neck gets all red. Can I rub on some of your pink face stuff sometime?"

The intimacy of the family altar can bring understanding and compassion and love for the people who are the dearest to us.

Isaiah 61:3 tells us of the "garment of praise" that God gives us in exchange for the "spirit of heaviness." What is your picture of that verse? Mine is of a beautiful, shimmering, chiffon dress contrasted with a heavy, black overcoat. Let's make the prayers of the family altar our "garment of praise."

7

Supplementary Ideas

*And these words, which I command thee this day,
shall be in thine heart. . . . And thou shalt bind
them for a sign upon thine hand, and they shall be
as frontlets between thine eyes. And thou shalt
write them upon the posts of thy house, and on thy
gates* (Deuteronomy 6:6, 8-9).

ALL THROUGH SCRIPTURE we see God's use of object
lessons to make truth live for His people. The rain-
bow coloring the sky after a storm is a sign of His
promise. His voice came to Moses from a burning
bush. The tabernacle pictured God's presence in the
lonely, frightening desert. He taught Jeremiah
through objects such as a cloth in Jeremiah 13; a
broken bottle in chapter 19; a yoke in chapter 27.
Jesus washed the disciples' feet as an object lesson
in humility; He used bread and wine to represent
His body and blood.

You can use this same principle in your devotions

to help all of you understand Scriptural truth. Pictures can convey a message when words fail and help us see what we sometimes do not hear. So be alert for anything that will illustrate the Scripture you are reading, the truth you are teaching, the needs of the people for whom you are praying. Pictures do not have to be colored and expertly framed; even the comic page in the newspaper has cartoons that illustrate scriptural truths. Be a magazine clipper—of pictures, anecdotes, cartoons. Do not throw out Sunday school papers until you have looked at them for every possible use. In fact do not throw them away at all—find someone who can use them.

Do keep one word of warning in mind. Be critical of the materials you use in your family devotions. Ask yourself, Does it really make the Scripture truth clear? Will my children remember only the picture or the object and not the idea behind it? Do not use anything that does not represent the Bible truth accurately. You cannot be sure that your explanation will be clear or that it will be understood the way you meant it to be. Look again at the age characteristics, and find how old children have to be before they can understand symbols. Do not let a misunderstood picture hinder them from growing spiritually.

You will find a few good object-lesson books. But as you live with your children, you will find object lessons around you every day. For example, in family devotions you are reading Matthew 5, where

Jesus speaks of salt. You could all sit around and agree that salt is important to food, and even little Bobby can say he thinks food is icky without salt. But if you do not salt any of the food you serve at dinner that evening, you can be sure everyone will be impressed by the force of the verses in Matthew.

Adults are familiar with the idea of scrolls, but children may not be. Illustrate how books used to look by helping the children make a scroll. If nothing else is available, just glue a couple of yards of white shelf-paper to two wooden rolling pins.

Anything that deepens the significance of your family altar is worth using. Just do not let the objects and handwork be only busywork that clutters a drawer for a while and then is thrown out. Be sure the projects and activities have educational value.

Ray and Peggy helped four-year-old Chrissie make a notebook of her Sunday school papers when she did not want to give them away. They used each Sunday's memory verse for that week's devotions. Chrissie pasted the Sunday school paper picture on one page, and under it Mother wrote the verse that went with the picture: "I am with you alway" (Matthew 28:20). Then, during the week, they looked for a picture that meant something to Chrissie—a picture of a little girl in bed at night—and pasted it on the opposite page.

Maybe you are thinking with some impatience of how much time this takes—time you do not have.

Look at it this way: if this helps give your children a shield in later years against "all the fiery darts of the wicked one" (Ephesians 6:16), then it is time well spent.

And anyway, you are not doing this all by yourself. If you are, it is not a family project. You may have to start some of the ideas and give your advice and some help; but the more your children do on their own, both with the ideas and the work, the more enthusiasm they will have, and the more they will learn.

You may object, too, that all these other activities will take away from the Bible and prayer time. Well, no—not if you do not let them. The actual reading of Scripture and the actual praying is the heart of the family altar. The other activities are only aids to understanding. Remember the salt illustration: that was to help understand truth, not detract from it.

Some of these extras will take time from the actual twenty minutes or half hour you spend together in family devotions. But if your family altar takes hold of your family life as you want it to, it will spill over naturally into other parts of the day.

Hopefully, your whole family has opportunities through your church for service such as visiting new families, hospital visiting, or singing in a nursing home. Because of this, you may not want to do as much of this as a family.

But do try as a family to build missionary interest,

so that your children will have a personal contact with a missionary family that maybe even a Sunday school class cannot give. Do not be satisfied with a "God bless the missionaries" attitude. "Adopt" a missionary family with children about the same age as yours. Write personal letters; remember them at Christmas and on their birthdays. This does not necessarily mean you must buy gifts, because sometimes duty is so high on packages that missionaries would rather not receive them.

When a missionary writes, "It's really hot here," or, "Our rainy season has started," find out what that means. Find out what "hot" means in Zaire or Indonesia or Vietnam and how long the rainy season is. This might have the side benefit of keeping down the grumbling when your kids have to wear raincoats to school for a couple of days in a row.

Buy a large map of Africa or whatever country your missionaries are in. You and the children together can spend a part of your family altar time finding out something about its history, its climate, what the flag looks like, whether it is mountainous, what the government is like, what happens to missionaries when there is a revolution in the country, what the people eat, where the children have to go to school. This is not just to fill up time in family devotions or satisfy idle curiosity. It is to help you to be informed when you pray for the situations your missionaries face.

Just be sure that whatever creative activities you use to make your family altar be a vital part of your lives results in making each member of the family a doer of the Word and not a hearer only (James 1: 22).

WHEN YOU MEMORIZE SCRIPTURE

Do you *have* to memorize Bible verses? Well, not if you do not think God's Word is important to know. But you do think it is, of course, and you want your children to hide it in their hearts. What is discouraging is how hard it is to get children to memorize—especially since you have always had the same problem of reluctance.

But memorizing can be fun, if you make it a family project. You may have to do a little arm-twisting on this to get started, and this arm-twisting may have to start with yourself. Think through the value of knowing scripture passages. Remember the time you visited your friend in the hospital and could not think of the right verse to give the help you knew she needed?

Remember the last time you went to the doctor for a checkup? How would you have felt if he had had to pull out his medical books to look up everything before he could report on your condition? You would not have had too much confidence in his ability. A lot of us are this way with the Bible; we know there is a verse somewhere that is just what we need—but we do not know where it is.

There is an even more important reason why we should memorize Scripture, given in Psalm 119:11: "Thy word have I hid in mine heart, that I might not sin against thee." We desperately need the Word of God as a guard against temptation. Your responsibility is to help your children develop the desire to memorize. When you have done that, you are on your way.

Talk about your feeling in family devotions and explain why you think memorizing Scripture is important. If you have not done much of it, be frank enough to say so. Throw out a discussion question: What would we do without a Bible? Suppose a knock came on the door, and a policeman was there to confiscate any Bible in the house, and then he burned them. (Acting out such a situation will make an even deeper impression.) But the question is, Could we replace the Bible from memory? Tom, could you write the Twenty-third Psalm from memory? Sue, what about the first two chapters of Genesis? Mom and Dad, could you together recite the book of Revelation?

In preparing for this discussion, write to a missionary organization like the Slavic Gospel Association for current information on what is happening in some countries where Christians have to read the

Bible in secret. Or read from a book like *God's Smuggler,* by Brother Andrew. Help your children see that what they take for granted is very precious to other people, and some die for their faith in God and His Word.

Now, of course, you are not going to memorize just to memorize. You will want what you learn to be valuable *now* as well as in some future emergency. So keep all your age levels and needs in mind. You may not meet every need with every verse you learn, but you will discover that many verses can be adapted to speak to each family member. The youngest can learn just part of a verse; "I will trust," out of Isaiah 12:2, is sufficient for the three-year-old. But the seven-year-old needs the additional truth that he can trust and not be afraid; and the junior adds the reason for his confidence, that it is based on God's power to help him.

Use every device possible to help yourselves memorize. Decide on a verse a day, and start learning it at breakfast, so that it will go to work and to school and around the house with each one. Type it on flash cards, and put one at each place at the table; or write it in large letters on one card, and prop it against the sugar bowl. Cut out letters, paste them on construction paper, and tape it to the refrigerator door; or type the verse on small slips of paper, and tape them to every mirror in the house. You will find many other ingenious ways to aid memorization.

Use contests, not to compete but to encourage. Give as much credit to tiny Barbie's accurate recital of "God is love" as you do to teenage Jim's memorizing of Psalm 91. Give rewards, if you want; don't worry about the dos and don'ts of "paying" children to memorize God's Word. The point is, it will be *there,* in their hearts, and you have helped them enjoy learning it.

Never laugh at mispronounced words, and do not scold; but do correct them. Insist on accuracy. It is much better to have a child learn a brief portion thoroughly than to half-stumble through many verses.

Choose some verses to memorize unitedly. Psalm 23 is a good portion to help you get started on this memory project. It is familiar to most of you, so you will not be striking out into brand new territory. Be sure to explain the verses as they are memorized. "The LORD is my shepherd, I shall not want," needs explaining so a child will not think it means, "I shall not want Him." This psalm is easy to visualize, and everyone can watch for pictures he thinks illustrate the verses. Ask everyone to either look for a picture or draw his own to show what "my cup runneth over" (v. 5) means. You may find some have totally mistaken ideas, and you will have a chance to explain the meaning of this verse and of others. Read the psalm aloud together in several different versions and paraphrases. Find it in song form in your hymn book, and sing it together; listen to different hymn arrangements of the psalm, from the beloved "Crimond" melody to the more contemporary tunes.

Whatever methods you use to aid in memorizing, remember these principles: (1) the verses must be understood; (2) the verses must be frequently repeated; (3) the verses must be practiced in life; (4) the verses must meet a need to grow.

Do not assume that because a child has rattled off a verse quickly he knows it. Help him to reinforce it frequently by living it. The best way to do this is by letting your children see *you* live the verses you learn. Do you "give thanks always"; "speak truth with your neighbor"; "let not the sun go down on your wrath"? Are you always "kind, tenderhearted, forgiving one another"? Saying and living must match, or verses have not really been learned. The great thing about God's Word is that as we get into it, it works in us and makes us able to live what we say.

Work out any kind of a memory program you think your family needs and can handle adequately. If you want more help and a definite system to follow, write to: Bible Memory Association, Box 12000, St. Louis, Mo., 63112.

Do not wait any longer to let memorizing Scripture put zest in your family altar.

WHEN YOU USE MUSIC

Singing together is a great way to share the "joy of the Lord" which God says is "our strength" (Nehemiah 8:10). Use music to give a lilt to your family worship.

If you are not particularly musical and are shy about singing in public, do not be at home. It is the place you can let go and make that "joyful noise" unto the Lord, and no one will laugh at you. It is the place to give your children a heritage of Gospel songs and hymns they will treasure all their lives. Use old ones, new ones, and even made-up ones if you want to.

A wide range of music will meet the tastes and musical ability of everyone. Include everything from "Jesus Loves Me, This I Know" or "This Little Light of Mine" to the majestic, "O God, Our Help in Ages Past," as well as Gospel songs, choruses, and hymns that cover the broad spectrum in between. Be open to new arrangements, and sing some of the contemporary songs.

Sing from your church hymnbook so everyone will have practice at home and then be familiar enough with the hymns to join enthusiastically in congregational singing. Use a hymn of the week or month, and try memorizing the words.

Find a Bible verse that fits the words of the hymns; you will discover that many songs are based on Scripture. Look in your Christian bookstore for books that tell the stories behind some of the well-known Gospel songs. Did you know that Mr. Spafford wrote "It Is Well with My Soul" after the tragic loss of his children when their ship sank in the Atlantic?

Build a record collection of hymns to listen to while you eat dinner; play those that will fit in with your family devotions for the evening. Have a singspiration evening now and then, and tape-record it. You could make a special tape of music to send to your missionary family.

As you use music in your family altar, you will find that some of the songs and choruses—old favorites as well as the new—are not scripturally correct or that they contain symbolism that is really nonsense. There is nothing wrong with nonsense, if it is labeled as such. But what does "Climb, Climb up Sunshine Mountain" really mean? Use your family-altar time to foster good judgment in your children. Do the words agree with what the Bible says? For instance, songs and hymns that speak of the Lord Jesus only as a good Example to follow are not really truthful; a good example cannot save anyone.

Do not come down with a heavy hand on either the words or the music if they are not to your liking. You are not there to stamp your tastes on the rest of the family but to help everyone develop the ability to think of "whatsoever things are true . . . honest . . . just . . . pure . . . lovely" (Philippians 4:8).

But perhaps you are concerned and troubled about the influence rock music is having on your children. You will need wisdom to tackle this, and the ability to speak about it calmly. Use all the loving, open communication you have established in other ways and about other subjects. In this, as in everything else you do with your children in family worship, do not nag or scold or argue. Remember God's promise to give the wisdom we need when we need it.

Now, maybe you think that rock music and the family altar are light-years apart. They are, of course. But rock music and your children may be closer together than you like to admit, and the beat and the words can have an evil effect. Be willing to listen to your children's viewpoint so they will listen to yours. Listen to some of the records and talk through the underlying meaning of the words. Compare the ideas with the scriptural truths you have been patiently teaching.

Center your activities and your thinking on God and His greatness. God knows the names of the trillions of stars and sees the fall of a tiny sparrow. We can be sure He knows about us and our children. He knows that we want to be able to follow the words of Psalm 150:6: "Let every thing that hath breath praise the LORD. Praise ye the LORD."

8

Seeing Results

Beloved, I wish above all things that thou mayest prosper and be in health, even as thy soul prospereth. For I rejoiced greatly, when the brethren came and testified of the truth that is in thee, even as thou walkest in the truth. I have no greater joy than to hear that my children walk in truth (3 John 2-4).

My HUSBAND quoted those words, with emphasis on the last sentence, when he took part in our son's ordination into the Christian ministry. Behind the words were all the years of loving, prayerful training during John's childhood when he accepted Christ as his Saviour, found God's will for his life as a seventh grader, and then walked in God's way through high school and college.

Parents want many things for their children: good health, a quick mind, adaptability to life, dependable friends, the right marriage partner. But all these are pale shadows compared to this prayer—that our children walk in truth, God's truth.

What can we expect the family altar to do? Let's stop and review. We have talked about two things: the *family*, defined as "parents and their children," and the *altar*, "an elevated place on which sacrifices are offered."

The earlier chapters discussed the things a family altar should do. For parents it should—

help them obey God in their personal living,
knit a close bond of love between husband and wife,
help them raise their children by God's commands,
keep them alert to their children's needs,
give new perspective on problems,
help them love their children,
reveal *their* need of God's help,
give Father the opportunity to be the spiritual leader of the home.

And for the children it is the place to—

learn of Jesus and His love for them,
receive instruction in righteousness,
be nourished in God's Word,
develop a love for spiritual things,
see a reason for obedience,
receive protection from unbelief and evil.

And it should help the family—

love one another,

have a better knowledge of the Bible,
learn to pray,
strengthen each one's personal convictions,
have questions and problems answered,
develop habits of personal holiness,
learn to worship God.

But none of these "shoulds" will result unless we want them to and are willing to work at them. Success comes from the eagerness we bring to the family worship and our willingness to put in the time and effort in spite of our demanding schedules.

"Thrown together" recipes are good only if the right ingredients are used in the right amounts. "Chocolate" mud cakes frosted with shiny sand *really* do not taste good! Patterns for clothes or crafts are planned and tested to be sure of exact specifications.

Dottie and I sat down one day to cut red construction-paper hearts for invitations to a valentine party. We talked while we worked and did not realize that we had used each newly cut heart, rather than the original, as the pattern for the next one. The further we departed from the pattern, the more misshapen our hearts became.

We are aiming for eternal results in family worship, so we want to use the right ingredients and cut from the original pattern. We have talked about using the Bible and prayer, about memorizing God's

Word as a family project, about using pictures and music and activities to illustrate and apply the truths of Scripture.

But you will want more help than we have been able to give in these brief chapters. This book is intended only to inspire you to start your family altar. So look for help from others who have been successful; talk to other families about what they do. Adapt what your church and Sunday school program offers. As you build your family altar, keep looking for ideas from books and other sources to help you grow and deepen your family's experiences. You can find many ideas, even if you do not follow them exactly. Here are some titles:

THE FAMILY

Adams, Jay E. *Christian Living in the Home*. Grand Rapids: Baker, 1972.

Brandt, Henry R., and Dowdy, Homer E. *Building a Christian Home*. Wheaton, Ill.: Scripture Press, 1960.

Brubaker, Omar, and Clark, Robert E. *Understanding People*. Wheaton, Ill.: ETTA, 1972.

Christenson, Larry. *The Christian Family*. Minneapolis: Bethany, 1970.

Dobson, James. *Dare to Discipline*. Wheaton, Ill.: Tyndale, 1970.

Epp, Theodore H. *Guidelines for Christian Parents*. Lincoln, Nebr.: Back to the Bible, 1967.

Hendricks, Howard. *Heaven Help the Home*. Wheaton, Ill.: Scripture Press, 1973.

Jacobsen, Marion Leach. *How to Keep Your Family Together and Still Have Fun*. Grand Rapids: Zondervan, 1972.

The Family Altar

Anson, Elva. *How to Keep the Family That Prays Together from Falling Apart*. Chicago: Moody, 1975.

Carlton, Anna Lee. *Guidelines for Family Worship*. Anderson, Ind.: Warner, 1964.

Jahsmann, Allen Hart, and Simon, Martin P. *Little Visits With God*. St. Louis, Mo.: Concordia, 1957.

LeBar, Lois E. *Family Devotions with School-age Children*. Old Tappan, N.J.: Revell, 1973.

Prime, Derek. *Tell Me About Becoming a Christian*. Chicago: Moody, 1969.

Soderholm, Marjorie E. *Explaining Salvation to Children*. Minneapolis: Free Church, 1962.

Bible Study Helps

Archer, Gleason. *A Survey of Old Testament Introduction*. Chicago: Moody, 1973.

Chafer, Lewis Sperry. *Major Bible Themes*. Rev. John F. Walvoord. Grand Rapids: Zondervan, 1974.

DeHaan, M. R. *Genesis and Evolution*. Grand Rapids. Zondervan, 1962.

Geisler, Norman L., and Nix, William E. *A General Introduction to the Bible*. Chicago: Moody, 1968.

Jensen, Irving L. *Independent Bible Study*. Chicago: Moody, 1963.

Little, Paul. *Know Why You Believe*. Downers Grove, Ill.: Inter-Varsity, 1968.

Mears, Henrietta C. *A Look at the Old Testament*. Glendale, Calif.: Gospel Light, 1967.

Richards, Lawrence O. *Creative Bible Teaching*. Chicago: Moody, 1970.

Vos, Howard F. *Effective Bible Study*. Grand Rapids: Zondervan, 1973.

ACTIVITIES

Doan, Eleanor. *Hobby Fun*. Grand Rapids: Zondervan, 1958.

Fischer, Howard. *Bible Tennis*. Chicago: Moody, 1973.

Sargent, John H. *Dynamic Object Talks*. Grand Rapids: Baker, 1955.

You have thrown a small stone into a quiet pond and watched the ripples it makes, haven't you? In a quiet pond the ripples spread out from the center where the stone went in, in ever widening circles. But it all started with the stone.

Individuals in your family and mine can be stones to influence first the family circle, then the neighborhood, the city, and the world, as our children establish homes with family altars and their children do the same. It takes only one family altar to begin the circles.

But there is that second word—*altar,* a place of sacrifice, a place of worship. Promoting family unity, developing family understanding, knowing more about the Bible, learning to pray—these goals blend into the main one, which is to worship God, giving ourselves to Him as a living sacrifice.

The Bible gives many illustrations of people of different ages, places, cultures, and experience, who had one thing in common: a vision of God which answered a definite need each had.

Think of Jacob—a young, spoiled, selfish son running away from a justly angry brother. He lay down to sleep in the empty desert and had a vision of a ladder that reached from heaven to earth. When he woke he exclaimed, "Surely the LORD is in this place!" (Genesis 28:16). And he worshiped God there.

We all know about Job, an immensely rich father who had raised a large family. In the midst of unexplained loss and suffering and the accusations of his friends, Job saw God's power and majesty in creation. And that was all the answer he needed to his, "Why am I suffering?" He said, "I have heard of thee by the hearing of the ear: but now mine eye seeth thee. Wherefore I abhor myself, and repent in dust and ashes" (Job 42:5-6).

Remember Isaiah, a godly prophet who had a tremendous vision of God. He saw the Lord sitting on a throne, with thousands of beings surrounding Him. Angels constantly served Him and spent their whole time saying, "Holy, holy, holy, is the LORD of hosts: the whole earth is full of his glory" (Isaiah 6:3). When Isaiah saw this magnificent sight, he responded: "Woe is me! for I am undone; because I am a man of unclean lips, and I dwell in the midst of a people of unclean lips: for mine eyes have seen the King, the LORD of hosts" (Isaiah 6:5).

Many years later, the apostle John, who had known the Lord Jesus intimately for three years on earth, saw Him glorified in a vision; and John fell at His feet in worship.

These responses do not come automatically or immediately, just because we have a family altar. Having family worship will not stop brother-sister squabbling at once, or eliminate disobedience and selfishness. It will not guarantee that you will always be calm when the six-year-old, while "helping," drops the jar of dill pickles on the freshly waxed kitchen floor. But it will help each of you "grow in grace" in all these daily situations.

Since I do not do needlework, I am always amazed to see how strands of varicolored yarn can blend together to make a pattern or a picture. I have a lovely basket of orange, yellow, and gold flowers our daughter embroidered for us when we moved into a new home. The tiny, exact stitches blend into a precise, perfect, beautiful picture.

At least, they do on the top. The bottom? Well, that is different; it is a mass of knots and clipped ends. But you see, they do not spoil the picture, because they cannot be seen.

Sometimes we see only the underside of our families. But God sees the finished picture, not finished by us but by His working. His aim is to present us perfect, "not having spot, or wrinkle, or any such thing"; one day we will be "holy and without blemish" (Ephesians 5:27). Let your family altar begin to develop men and women whose

> delight is in the law of the LORD; and in his law doth he meditate day and night. And he shall be like a tree planted by the rivers of water, that bringeth forth his fruit in his season; his leaf also shall not wither; and whatsoever he doeth shall prosper (Psalm 1:2-3).